# THE MUSLIM WOMAN'S PARTICIPATION IN SOCIAL LIFE

WOMEN'S EMANCIPATION DURING THE PROPHET'S LIFETIME

# THE MUSLIM WOMAN'S PARTICIPATION IN SOCIAL LIFE

## Volume 2

Abd al-Halim Abu Shuqqah

*Translated and Edited by*
Adil Salahi

KUBE
PUBLISHING

*The Muslim Woman's Participation in Social Life*

First published in England by
Kube Publishing Ltd
Markfield Conference Centre,
Ratby Lane, Markfield,
Leicestershire, LE67 9SY,
United Kingdom
Tel: +44 (0) 1530 249230
Fax: +44 (0) 1530 249656
Email: info@ kubepublishing.com
Website: www.kubepublishing.com

WOMEN'S EMANCIPATION DURING THE PROPHET'S LIFETIME



CIP data for this book is available from the British Library.

ISBN: 978-1-84774-152-3 *Paperback*
ISBN: 978-1-84774-153-0 *Ebook*

*Translate and Edit by*: Adil Salahi
*Cover Design by*: Nasir Cadir
*Typeset by*: nqaddoura@hotmail.com
*Printed by*: Elma Printing, Turkey

## Contents

## CHAPTER 4: Muslim Women's Participation in Social Life During the Prophet's Lifetime

# Transliteration Table

**Consonants. Arabic**

**initial, unexpressed, medial and final:** ء ʾ

| | | | | | | | |
|---|---|---|---|---|---|---|---|
| ا | a | د | d | ض | ḍ | ك | k |
| ب | b | ذ | dh | ط | ṭ | ل | l |
| ت | t | ر | r | ظ | ẓ | م | m |
| ث | th | ز | z | ع | ʿ | ن | n |
| ج | j | س | s | غ | gh | هـ | h |
| ح | ḥ | ش | sh | ف | f | و | w |
| خ | kh | ص | ṣ | ق | q | ي | y |

*Vowels, diphthongs, etc.*

| | | | | | | |
|---|---|---|---|---|---|---|
| short: | ـَ | a | ـِ | i | ـُ | u |
| long: | ـَا | ā | ـُو | ū | ـِي | ī |
| diphthongs: | | | ـَوْ | aw | | |
| | | | ـَيْ | ay | | |

# Introduction

## On Women's Participation in Social Life in Mixed Society

Muslim women are partners of Muslim men in building the best and purest human life on earth. God's Messenger (peace be upon him) states the truth as he says: 'Women are men's full sisters.' Therefore, a Muslim woman needs to play a serious part in all areas of life. Since life activities normally involve men, and in fact men play the major part in most such activities, Islam does not forbid Muslim women to meet men. Nor does it forbid that men and women see each other, talk to each other, or cooperate in doing something together, as long as Islamic values are maintained. Such meetings should be serious, without affectation, complication or sensitivity. In fact, women's participation in social life, which naturally involves the meeting of men and women, is the method approved of by Islam and established by God's Messenger (peace be upon him). He was certainly aware that such participation and mixing makes life easier and allows cooperation in what is good, while the opposite causes hardship and often leads to negative results. However, such participation was never meant to cause the Muslim woman any difficulty in the fulfilment of her primary responsibility towards her home and family. On the contrary, it helps in the development of her character so that she can better attend to that primary responsibility as well as others that she may have to fulfil towards her family or society.

Women's participation in social life and their meeting with men, whether it comes naturally or planned, to attend to some good task, was a common feature of Muslim society, in both public and private fields. Meeting in the public field includes:

- In the mosque: where obligatory prayers, funeral prayers or prayer at the time of an eclipse are held;
- Learning circles: wherever they are held, be it a mosque, prayer place or in a scholar's home;
- The Grand Mosque at the Ka'bah which God has made a resort for mankind and a sanctuary, so that people may perform the duties of hajj and *'umrah*;
- Places of Eid celebration, including the prayer place where women attend the Eid Prayer and glorify God together with men. This also includes the open area next to the mosque where the Abyssinians performed their show during the Prophet's lifetime;
- At a court of justice: whether this is held in the mosque or elsewhere. Men and women may be the parties to a dispute. A man may have to exchange vows with his wife;
- Attending funerals: including offering condolences, offering the Funeral Prayer, and accompanying the bereaved family in the funeral procession, but without going to the graveyard;
- Participation in jihad: women fulfil a supporting role behind the lines of engagement; cooking for the soldiers, providing

drinks, attending to the wounded and then transporting the casualties;

- At the place where two parties pray for God's judgement between them: just as God's Messenger intended to make this humble prayer with the Najran delegation, praying to God to judge in their dispute.

In the private sphere, men and women often meet and talk together, whether in homes during a visit, an invitation to a meal, requesting a favour, giving a gift, visiting an ill person, offering condolences or supporting in cases of distress. Private meetings outside the home occur when sharing in a public event, enjoining some good action, offering a service, making a proposal, doing some professional work or taking part in a political activity.

When men and women meet, observing the Islamic standards of propriety and decency, they take part in a healthy activity which is today called 'legitimate mixing.' This refers to the Muslim woman exercising an active, serious, goodly and pure life. Meeting men is an essential aspect of such a life. All forms of meeting encouraged by desire and pleasure are excluded, while forms of serious meeting are approved of, whether they occur naturally as part of life's flow, or are deliberately intended in order to achieve or do some good. Since both meeting and separating from the other sex are acceptable in Islam, it is serious, active and goodly life that indicates to the Muslim woman, in every situation and at each time, whether it is better to stay away from men or meet them. This means that the Muslim woman does not deliberately meet men to enjoy their company; for this is unlawful in Islam. What she aims at is to exercise an active and goodly life, whether this means meeting men or staying away from them.

Like marriage, participation and meeting men are normal practices of human life, which means that they have been part of human association ever since the start of human life. God created men and women so that they together build life on earth. Life cannot continue vigorously, and smoothly, unless we put this into practice. The conduct of prophets and God's messengers confirms this. In his own practice, Prophet Muhammad (peace be upon him) followed the same course as earlier prophets. Indeed, he opened it up so that it became applicable in all fields of life. At the same time, essential controls have been put in place to ensure that this practice continues without a blemish being cast on a pure and healthy Islamic life.

Thus, the Muslim woman approaches life with the light of God's guidance. The practical examples that we cite in this volume are merely examples of the implementation of this divine guidance, associated with certain verses of the Qur'an or hadiths. Besides, if all types of implementation exercised by believing women during the lifetimes of all prophets were to be recorded and classified, they would only remain some types of implementing God's guidance, while the scope of implementation remains much wider, both in our present time and throughout all generations. Divine guidance allows many, many more ways of implementation that could arise to suit each generation and society.

I would like to repeat here what I said in the Introduction to this work, as this may serve as a reminder and mind opener:

> The advocacy of the permissibility of leaving women's faces uncovered, and their participation in social life together with men and within Islamic ethics, after having established its permissibility with clear evidence, is also a call to sound guidance. Divine guidance aims to lift hardship from people. God says in the Quran: "He has laid no hardship on you in [anything that pertains to] religion." (22: 78). My call here is addressed to two groups of people:

**The first group** is composed of people who claim that it is forbidden for a woman to uncover her face and forbid all forms of participation in social life, regardless of the strong need for such participation or its being guided by Islamic morality. I call on this group to make sure of Islamic rulings and to beware of what the Prophet has warned against as he says: "A person who forbids what is lawful is like one who makes lawful what God has forbidden." Both transgress against God's law. When the Prophet guided Muslim women to leave their faces uncovered and to participate in social life, he only wanted what is best for the Muslim community. Muslims are thus able to progress in every good way in life. He also opened the way for Muslim women to undertake gainful employment, beginning with seeking education, teaching, helping her husband who may not be able to earn enough, and to participate in useful social activity, or positive political activity that aims to consolidate what is good and oppose deviation.

I follow an exemplary lead in explaining Islamic law to this group, as this lead is provided by 'Alī ibn Abi Ṭālib. One day, he offered the Ẓuhr Prayer and then sat down in the main square of Kufah, attending to people's needs until the 'Aṣr Prayer was due. He was brought some water, and he drank, washed his face, hands, head and feet. He then stood up and drank the rest of the water standing. He then said: "Some people dislike drinking in the standing position, but God's Messenger (peace be upon him) did the same as I have just done."

Ibn Ḥajar said: "'Alī's hadith includes very interesting points. One of these is that if a scholar finds people avoiding something which he knows to be permissible, he should explain to them the right way about it, lest time passes and people start to think that it is forbidden. If this is feared, the scholar should take the initiative and inform people of the correct ruling, even if he is not asked about it. If he is asked, this becomes even more strongly incumbent on him."

**The second group** is that of people who contravene God's law through permissive practices and unrestricted mixing. I call on these to obey God and to commit themselves only to what He has permitted. This means that they must cover what God has ordered to be covered, and that they should observe the Islamic code that regulates the meeting of men and women. Otherwise, they run the risk of incurring God's displeasure. They would also expose themselves to many of the social ills Western society suffers from.

Having said that, I draw the attention of this second group in particular to the fact that I have devoted the second chapter of this volume to the discussion of the Islamic standards of decency that apply to the participation of women. Such standards are the basic control that ensures that all types of participation are heedful of divine teachings. Taking heed of these teachings ensures the fine results of such participation.

To both groups I reconfirm that a woman's first and most important responsibility is to take care of her home and family. I hope this will put an end to any confusion that may occur through a hasty consideration of my repeated talk about women's emancipation, work and participation in social and political activity. These are serious matters and we do not approach them casually, or to appease advocates of Westernisation. We discuss them on the basis of God's Book and His Messenger's Sunnah. In other words, we discuss them in the light of religious texts and their clear and apparent import. We do not look for subtle connotations on which people normally differ. Our discussion of such issues is based on their Islamic concepts and remains within Islamic manners and limits. We do not refrain from using a word or words that are used by people who have different perspectives. Words remain part of our language. We do not discard them simply because other people load them with connotations that they do not have. On the contrary, we feel that we should revert these words to their original meanings, using them always in their true sense so that they regain their true import and all falsehood is seen in its true colour. Thus, the fabricators will have no leg to stand on.

To say that taking care of the family home is the first and most important responsibility of the woman means several things:

- Every individual, man or woman, needs to live in a happy family where mutual care and cooperation are well established. Human society is built on such families. The protection of the family – from the point of view of maintaining mutual love, care and cooperation between its members, as also taking good care of its young ones – is something that requires contributions by all individuals as well as civil and government institutions. The better this task is fulfilled the more man and woman achieve fulfilment and society progresses. To ignore such protection leads to the loss of both man and woman and the weakness of society.
- Both man and woman have their respective tasks in taking care of the home and the family, but their tasks differ in nature. The fact that the woman's primary responsibility is to take care of her home and family does not mean that there are no other responsibilities which may differ according to the circumstances of the family and the needs of society. Yet the care of the home and the family always has top priority, particularly when there is conflict between responsibilities.

- The claim of an inevitable conflict between responsibilities is a false one, based on a misconception or on the man's or woman's weakness. It may also be the result of the man's selfishness or the lack of ability by public institutions. In our study we try – seeking God's help – to clear misconceptions and to map out the way that deals with weakness and inability. We then show the feasibility of coordination and the possibility of achieving a healthy balance between responsibilities in most scenarios, particularly when this is coupled with giving working women more advantages in professional work. In all this, we endeavour to protect the primary responsibility from being undermined in any way, yet also seek to protect other vital interests achieved through other responsibilities. Both husband and wife, the systems operated by the government or social institutions and also the traditions upheld by society must all endeavour to achieve proper coordination between primary and secondary responsibilities. If such perfect co-ordination proves impossible to achieve, despite persistent efforts, the primary responsibility should then be given its due care and priority, attending to other responsibilities as far as possible, even if in a limited way, so that the benefits that such responsibilities bring about are not totally lost or ignored. We should always remember that our Muslim society cannot be well built and cannot achieve the highest grades of power and civilisation unless we benefit by the fruits of all these tasks and responsibilities. Only then can we deserve the Qur'anic description: 'You are the best community ever raised for mankind.' (3: 110)
- Some men persist in their wrong understanding of Islamic law and remain prey to a feeling that they must possess their women. They refuse to allow her to do any task outside the home, even if it is for the benefit of the home or the community. We can do no more for such people than illustrating, as far as we can, the teachings of Islam. We refer

these men/this group to the third volume in this series which is devoted to women's participation in professional work and social and political activities.

In conclusion of this Introduction we list the headings of the chapters related to women's participation in social work stated by Imam al-Bukhari in his *Ṣaḥīḥ* anthology of authentic hadiths. It is enough to peruse these headings to realise that such participation is part of the Prophet's sunnah. May God shower mercy on Imam al-Bukhari, as scholars say that his profound *fiqh* insight is reflected in the headings he wrote for his chapters:

**Book of Knowledge:**

- Chapter: The imam's duty to admonish and educate women.
- Chapter: Should a day be devoted especially to women's education?

**Book of Prayer:**

- Chapter: Women sleeping in the mosque.
- Chapter: Women attending the mosque at night and in darkness.
- Chapter: Women pray behind men.
- Chapter: Early departure by women after Fajr Prayer.
- Chapter: Should a woman seek her husband's permission to go to the mosque?

**Book of Friday:**

- Chapter: Should women, children and others attending Friday Prayer have a bath beforehand?

**Book of the Eid:**

- Chapter: Women, including those in menstruation, should attend the prayer place.

- Chapter: The imam should admonish women on Eid Day.
- Chapter: If a woman does not have a top garment on Eid Day.
- Chapter: Women in menstruation stay behind the prayer place.

**Chapters on the Eclipse:**

- Chapter: Women to pray with men during the eclipse.

**Chapters on action during Prayer:**

- Chapter: Women clap.

**Book of Funerals:**

- Chapter: A man says: 'Remain patient' to a woman standing by a grave.
- Chapter: Women following funerals.

**Book of *Tarāwīḥ* Prayer:**

- Chapter: Women's *i'tikāf*
- Chapter: *I'tikāf* by a bleeding woman
- Chapter: A woman visiting her husband during his *i'tikāf*.

**Book of Sales:**

- Chapter: Buying and selling with women.

**Book of Jihad:**

- Chapter: The call on men and women to take part in jihad and seek martyrdom.
- Chapter: Women's jihad.
- Chapter: Women joining a maritime expedition.
- Chapter: A man taking his wife on a military expedition but not his other women.
- Chapter: Women join men in jihad and fighting.

- Chapter: Women carrying water for men in battle.
- Chapter: Women treating wounded soldiers.
- Chapter: Women returning the wounded and the dead.

**Book of the Obligatory Five Prayers:**

- Chapter: Protection extended by women.

**Book of explaining the Qur'an:**

- Chapter: 'When believing women come as migrants.'
- Chapter: 'When believing women come and pledge to you.'

**Book of Marriage:**

- Chapter: A man says to his brother: Choose either of my two wives.
- Chapter: A woman offering herself in marriage to a devout man.
- Chapter: Supplication for the women who prepare the bride and for the bride.
- Chapter: Women preparing a bride for her husband.
- Chapter: Women and children going to a wedding.
- Chapter: A woman attends to men's needs at a wedding and personally serves them.
- Chapter: No man may be alone with a woman except one who is unlawful for her to marry [i.e. *maḥram*], and visiting one whose husband is absent.
- Chapter: It is unlawful for a man to be alone with a woman at other people's places.
- Chapter: A woman looking at foreigners without suspicion.
- Chapter: Women going out to attend to their needs.

**Book of Patients:**

- Chapter: Women visiting sick men.

**Book of Medicine:**

- Chapter: Can a man treat a woman, or a woman treat a man?
- Chapter: A woman to supplicate for the recovery of a man.

**Book of Seeking Permission:**

- Chapter: Men greeting women and women greeting men.

This is a complete list of the headings of chapters in al-Bukhari's *Ṣaḥīḥ*, related to women's participation in social life and their meetings with men.

# CHAPTER I

## Reasons for Muslim Women's Participation in Social Life during the Revelation of the Islamic Message

CHAPTER SUMMARY:

- To Make Life Easy
- Women's Character Development
- Pursuit of Knowledge
- Doing Good
- Enjoining Right and Forbidding Evil
- Islamic Advocacy
- Participation in Jihad
- Professional Work
- Political Activity
- Facilitating Marriage
- Facilitating Relaxation, Attending Celebrations and Good Activities
- New Social Aspects Requiring More Participation

# *Reasons for Muslim Women's Participation in Social Life during the Revelation of the Islam Message*

We do not have any text in the Qur'an or Hadith that specifies the aims of women's participation in the social life of the Muslim community or intercommunication between men and women. However, we can easily deduce these from texts and reports of numerous events and occasions where such participation occurred. On the basis of such texts, i.e. Qur'anic verses and authentic hadiths, we will outline the most important reasons and aims for such participation.

## 1. To Make Life Easy

Islam aims to build a good, pure and clean social life which must always maintain good progress, steering away from difficulty and hardship. It wants its followers, men and women, to approach life with ease and serenity. In all matters, religious and secular, Muslims look up to the Prophet for guidance. On the question of an easy approach to life in general, 'Ā'ishah said: "Whenever the Prophet had two options to choose from, he chose the easier one, unless it involved disobedience of God. If it did, he would steer far away from it." (Related by al-Bukhari and Muslim)

During the Prophet's time, women used to go to the Prophet with their questions, or whenever they needed something. They did not ask their husbands or male relatives to do this for them. A man might have been too busy, or unwilling, or might not have seen the importance of the question, or might have been unable to fully understand and deliver the question or the answer. It was easier for everybody, then, for a woman who had a question to go to the Prophet herself, even though she would meet men there, as the Prophet was often in the company of his companions. We will quote some examples:

Buraydah narrated: "I was sitting with the Prophet when a woman came to him and said: 'I gave my mother a slave woman, but my mother has now died. [What is her position now?]' The Prophet said: 'Your reward is confirmed and you now regain the slave woman through inheritance...'" (Related by Muslim)

Ibn 'Abbās narrated: "A woman from the tribe of Juhaynah asked the Prophet: 'My mother made a pledge to God to offer the hajj, but she did not do so before death overtook her. Shall I do the hajj on her behalf?' The Prophet said: 'Yes! Do it on her behalf...'" (Related by al-Bukhari)

Fāṭimah bint Qays reports that she was married to Abu 'Amr ibn Ḥafṣ ibn al-Mughīrah. When he divorced her for the third time she went to the Prophet asking his ruling on her leaving her home. He ordered that she move to the home of Ibn Umm Maktūm, a blind man. (Related by Muslim)

Sometimes men asked their wives to speak to the Prophet and put questions to him. One example is reported by Zaynab, ʿAbdullāh ibn Masʿūd's wife: "Zaynab used to support her husband and some orphans under her care. She said to ʿAbdullāh, her husband: 'Ask God's Messenger whether it is acceptable that I should support you and my orphans out of my zakat?' He said to her: 'Go and ask the Prophet yourself.' She went out to put her question to the Prophet..." (Related by al-Bukhari and Muslim)

This incident brings to mind a rather unusual story related by Imam Ahmad ibn Ḥanbal in his hadith anthology, *al-Musnad*: an Ansari man sent his wife to ask the Prophet a question which would have been better asked by a man. When his wife brought him the answer, he was not satisfied, and he sent her to ask him again, pointing out further details. Neither the man nor his wife felt any embarrassment. Moreover, to make things easy for people, the Prophet did not object to the woman coming to ask him when her husband was at home. The hadith in question goes as follows:

ʿAṭā' narrated: "A man from the Anṣār kissed his wife when he was fasting. Following his instructions, his wife asked the Prophet about this. The Prophet told her that he, i.e. God's Messenger, does so. The woman told her husband the answer, but he said to her: 'The Prophet may be given concessions in some areas. Go back to him and find out.' She went back to the Prophet and said that her husband felt that the Prophet might have special concessions. The Prophet said: 'I am the most God-fearing person among you and I know best the limits set by God...'" (Related by Ahmad)

It is indeed as ʿĀ'ishah said: the Prophet led the way in making things easier for the Muslim community in all situations. If social mixing between men and women and their frequent contact made life easier, but for which there were some impediments preventing it, he would show the way out which ensured that life was put back on an easy course. The following example is reported by Jābir ibn ʿAbdullāh:

"My maternal aunt was divorced. She wanted to go to her farm to gather the fruit of her date trees. A man reproached her for so going out during her waiting period. She went to the Prophet and asked him about this. He said: 'Yes, you can go out to gather your dates. When doing so, you may give something for charity or do some other good work.'" (Related by Muslim)

Another example is reported by al-Ṭabarī on Qatādah's authority: "The Prophet specified (in the conditions of the pledge of loyalty given by women) that they would not wail for their dead relatives, and that they would not talk to men. ʿAbd al-Raḥmān ibn ʿAwf said: 'We may have guests and we may be away from our women.' The Prophet said: 'I do not mean those.'" The Prophet's answer shows that he did not mean talking seriously to trusted men. He only meant frivolous talking to unworthy men. It should be noted here that ʿAbd al-Raḥmān ibn ʿAwf, a truly God-fearing companion of the Prophet, raised an important point: it would be very hard for women not to speak to men who may arrive as guests and especially when these women might happen to be on their own. The Prophet's answer ensured that no hardship was left unremoved.

## 2. Women's Character Development

When women participate fully in the social life of the Muslim community, meeting men on an equal basis, they have the chance to attend to much that is good, adopt higher concerns and gain useful experience. We will gain a better insight into these areas when we speak about other issues such as pursuing education, doing useful work, and participating in jihad. By contrast, when women are kept away from society, they will be deprived of all such experience and they will only have petty concerns. Even in the best conditions under such overall confinement, women would be denied better and more beneficial alternatives. For example, women who want to be educated will be denied access to a capable male teacher and forced to study under one of his female students. They cannot participate in open discussions, but are instead allowed only a limited scope for discussion. What we claim, then, is that social mixing with men helps in the development of women's characters. When a woman meets pious men, her own piety is nurtured; when she meets scholars, her knowledge grows; and meeting social and political activists increases her own social and political awareness.

No one denies that such character development is also achieved when women meet other women who are pious, scholars, or socially and politically active. We all know, however, that in our Muslim societies, the highest positions in all these areas are monopolised by men. How, then, can we help women to develop their piety and increase their scholarship and awareness of their society? We are speaking here about women in general, not the privileged few who belong to families that are rich with such expertise. The only way is to allow women to participate with men in their best meeting places. What is important is to ensure that in such meeting places all concentrate on serious talk and fruitful action, in all areas of piety, scholarship and social and political activity.

During the Prophet's lifetime, a measure of all this was ensured by women frequenting the Prophet's mosque in Madinah, which was the centre from which Muslim men and women received their religious, cultural and social education. Therefore, when a woman went out to attend a function where she could listen to the Qur'an or the Prophet's directives, attend a lecture or a seminar, or to meet other Muslim women with whom she could cooperate in doing something useful, she would certainly be doing well. The greater measure in the first Muslim community was provided by the Prophet's wives who benefited by their close association with the man who delivered God's message to mankind, and who emanated knowledge to all people. At the same time, the Prophet's wives were full participants in the life of the community and active within it. They were, thus, able to attain a high standard of knowledge. They became teachers from whom the most eminent figures among the Prophet's companions and their successors learnt much, in all disciplines of Hadith, *Fiqh* and the interpretation of the Qur'an.

Our scholars today should follow the Prophet's example as he made sure of addressing the women himself, not assigning the task to any of his noble companions. In his authentic hadith anthology, al-Bukhari makes a special reference to this point by quoting 'Aṭā', one of the eminent scholars of the *tābi'īn* generation, i.e. the one immediately following the Prophet's companions. 'Aṭā' was asked whether the imam should go to address the assembled women when he had finished, as the Prophet used to do at the end of the Eid Prayer. He answered: "This is an obligation they must fulfil. I wonder why they are not doing it."

Our women should also follow the example set by the early Muslim women when they went to the Prophet asking him about whatever they needed to know. They did not leave the matter to their fathers or husbands. Indeed, many felt that they needed to ask the Prophet himself, rather than put their questions to his wives for answer. It is useful to recall here Subay'ah's story when she went and asked the Prophet whether she could marry after she had delivered her baby, shortly after becoming a widow. She was not sure of what Abu al Sanābil told her that she needed to wait the full term of widows, which is four months and ten days. Commenting on this story, Ibn Ḥajar says: "It shows Subay'ah's intelligence and clarity of purpose as she was reluctant to accept Abu al-Sanābil's ruling. She felt that she must have a clear ruling by the Prophet himself." Moreover, our women should follow in the footsteps of the Prophet's wives, so as to help some of them attain the highest degree of scholarship so that they can become teachers of men and women alike.

It is useful to mention a couple of examples of women who attained a high standard of intellectual and social ability as a result of their participation in the social life of the Muslim community, mixing with God's Messenger and his companions.

i. Umm Sulaym

Umm Sulaym was a woman whom the Prophet frequently visited. Anas ibn Mālik, her son, reports: "When the Prophet passed close to Umm Sulaym's place, he dropped in to greet her." (Related by al-Bukhari)

She sent the Prophet gifts on joyful occasions. Anas narrated: "God's Messenger got married and consummated his marriage. My mother cooked *ḥays* [a dish made of dried milk, dates and butter] and put it in a stone jug. She said: 'Anas, take this to God's Messenger and say: my mother has sent this to you with her greetings, and she says that this is too little from us to you, Messenger of God.'"

She also played hostess to the Prophet and a large number of his companions. Anas reports: "...The Prophet said to her: 'Come on Umm Sulaym! Bring what you have.' She brought the bread she had, and the Prophet instructed his companions to cut it into small pieces. She also brought what she had of butter and honey and mixed it [to serve with the bread]... They all ate their fill despite their numbering 70 or 80 men." (Related by al-Bukhari and Muslim)

Furthermore, she used to go with the Prophet on his jihad expeditions. Anas reports: "When the Prophet went on an expedition, Umm Sulaym and some of the Anṣār women went out with him, giving the soldiers water to drink and attending to the wounded." (Related by Muslim)

It is not surprising, then, that she should set a great example for a mother who had just had the distressing experience of losing her son. In order to lessen the effect on her husband, she broke the news to him in this way: "Abu Ṭalḥah! Should some people lend an article to their neighbours, then the borrowers are asked to return it, can they refuse?" He said: "No. They cannot." She said to him, "Then accept the loss of your child." (Related by Muslim) Imam al-Nawawī, who wrote a commentary on Muslim's anthology of authentic hadiths, comments on how she broke the news to her husband: "Giving the example of a borrowed article shows her as a woman of broad knowledge and great faith." No wonder then that the Prophet once said, "I dreamt that I went into heaven and there I found al-Rumayṣā', Abu Talhah's wife." (Related by al-Bukhari and Muslim)

ii. Asmā' bint 'Umays

Asmā' bint 'Umays travelled with the male companions of the Prophet on their first migration from Makkah to Abyssinia. Abu Mūsā al-Ash'arī said: "Asmā' was one of [the Prophet's companions] who came with us [to Madinah]. She had migrated to Abyssinia along with those who migrated there." (Related by al-Bukhari and Muslim)

She then migrated to Madinah. After she settled in Madinah, she frequently met the Prophet and many of his companions. Abu Mūsā narrated: "... Asmā' bint 'Umays visited Ḥafṣah, the Prophet's wife... 'Umar came in while Asmā' was there. He asked [his daughter]: 'Who is this?' She said: 'Asmā' bint 'Umays.' 'Umar said: 'The Abyssinian one? The seafarer one?' Asmā' said: 'Yes.' He said: 'We migrated ahead of you. Therefore, we have more claim to God's Messenger than you. When the Prophet came in, she said: 'Prophet of God! 'Umar said this and that.' He said: 'What did you say to him?' She said: 'I said such-and-such.' He said: 'He does not have more claim to me than you. He and his companions have one migration, while you, the boat travellers, have two migrations.' She said: 'I saw Abu Mūsā and the people of the boat coming to me, group after group, asking me about this hadith.'"

When her first husband, Ja'far ibn Abi Ṭālib, died she continued to meet men after her second marriage to Abu Bakr. She nursed Abu Bakr during his illness and he was visited by a large number of people whilst she was with him all the time. Asmā' was a woman of high intelligence and courage. When 'Umar, who was held in awe by most men, teased her, she argued with him both in jest and seriously. It is no wonder that she was sought in marriage by the most noble among the Prophet's companions, marrying first Ja'far, then Abu Bakr and finally 'Alī ibn Abi Ṭālib. May God be pleased with them all.

### 3. Pursuit of Knowledge

The pursuit of knowledge is an Islamic duty God requires every Muslim to fulfil so that life in this world can be set aright and success is achieved in the life to come. This duty applies to every Muslim woman in the same way as it applies to every Muslim man. For a Muslim, man or woman, life in this world is the time when the ground is prepared, seeds are planted and trees and other plants are attended to, while the life to come is the harvest season. When Muslims dedicate themselves to build a sound and healthy human life on earth, they receive their full reward on the Day of Judgement. Islam urges Muslims to pursue knowledge, addressing all its instructions to both men and women, as in the following examples:

Anas quotes God's Messenger as saying: "The pursuit of knowledge is a duty that applies to every Muslim." (Related by al-Bayhaqī)

Abu al-Dardā' narrated that God's Messenger (peace be upon him) said: "Whoever sets on a way to pursue knowledge God will set him on a way leading to heaven. Angels lower their wings for the pursuer of knowledge as a gesture of approval." (Related by Ahmad)

When we speak of Islamic knowledge which alerts and enlightens our minds and hearts, we wonder how anyone can achieve such knowledge without meeting scholars and studying under them? We read how the early Muslim women were keen to meet the Prophet so as to receive knowledge from this most primary source. Then, after the Prophet had passed away, men of the first two Islamic generations frequently sought knowledge from its next richest source, the Prophet's wives. Since this early period was the model to be followed, Muslim men and women should continue to seek knowledge from its highest sources and best scholars, be they men or women. No man or woman should refrain from learning from the best teachers on account of the teacher's sex or if the instructor is female.

Indeed, the Prophet's female companions asked him to devote a special session for them. Abu Sa'īd al-Khudrī narrated: "A woman said to the Prophet: 'Messenger of God! Men have taken most of your discourse. Could you allocate a special day for us?' He said to her: 'Assemble on such and such a day...' When they assembled, he went to speak to them..." (Related by al-Bukhari and Muslim) We must remember here that when women asked the Prophet for their own session, they did not object to being in the same session with men. Rather, they were keen to have the added privilege whereby they could have their own special discourse in addition to their participation with men in the Prophet's mosque. When the Prophet allocated this special day for women, they continued to come to the mosque, sharing with men in all that the Prophet taught.

This keen desire to pursue knowledge enabled such early Muslim women to question male scholars among the Prophet's companions concerning their rulings. ʿAbdullāh ibn Masʿūd once said: "Expelled from God's grace are those women who make tattoos for others, or seek to have tattoos made for them, and those who thin their eyebrows, and those who seek to appear more beautiful by changing God's creation." Umm Yaʿqūb, a woman from the Asad clan, heard of this statement and went to see him. She said: "I heard that you have cursed such and such women?" He replied: "Why would I not curse the ones God's Messenger had cursed and what is in God's Book?" She re-joined: "I have read the Qur'an from cover to cover and I cannot find what you have said." He replied: "Had you really read it, you would have found it. Have you not read God's order: 'Whatever God's Messenger gives you, take it; and whatever he forbids you, refrain from it?'" She said: "Yes." He said: "God's Messenger has certainly forbidden us that." She said: "But I see that your wife does it." He said: "Go and look at her yourself." She went to see his wife, but she found that his wife did nothing of this. He commented: "Had my wife been doing any such thing, I would not associate with her." (Related by al-Bukhari and Muslim)

By contrast, Muslim men sought to learn the Prophet's practice from his wives. Anas ibn Mālik reports: "Three men came to the Prophet's homes asking his wives about his voluntary worship..." (Related by al-Bukhari and Muslim)

We also read that when male scholars differed on a question of Islamic law, they could refer to women for further knowledge. Ṭāwūs said: "I was with ʿAbdullāh ibn ʿAbbās when Zayd ibn Thābit asked him: 'Have you ruled that a female pilgrim who is in her waiting period could depart from Makkah without having performed the *ṭawāf* of farewell?' Ibn ʿAbbās said: 'If you disagree, ask this Anṣārī woman [naming her] whether the Prophet instructed her to do so.' Zayd came back later and said to Ibn ʿAbbās: 'I realize that what you said is indeed true.'" (Related by Muslim)

## 4. Doing Good

Indeed, social mixing between men and women can facilitate doing good. Umm Sharīk was a rich woman from the Anṣār who spent much of her money for God's cause and was very hospitable to her guests. Her home was like a welfare centre. Fāṭimah bint Qays reports: "... the Prophet told me to move to Umm Sharīk's home. I said that I would do so. He then changed his mind and said to me: 'Do not do that. Umm Sharīk receives numerous guests.'" (Related by Muslim)

Their acquisition of knowledge enabled early Muslim women to do what was necessary to ensure the removal of any impediment that prevented good action. Asmā' bint Abu Bakr was married to al-Zubayr, one of the earliest Muslims who was very close to the Prophet, but she realised that her husband was rather jealous in respect of his wife. Therefore, when she felt that his jealousy could prevent something good coming to other people, she tried cleverly to overcome his predilection, as appears in this story which she herself reports: "A man came to me and said: 'Umm 'Abdullāh, I am a poor man and I want to have a corner next to your home where I could sell things.' I said: 'If I allow you to do so, al-Zubayr will refuse. Therefore, come back and ask me in his presence.' He came back later and repeated his request in front of my husband. I said: 'You cannot find in the whole of Madinah any place other than my home?' Al-Zubayr said to me: 'Why would you prevent a poor man from selling things?' Thus, the man started his trade and did well." (Related by Muslim) Had it not been for Asmā's clever device, her husband's jealousy might have prevented the man from setting up shop in front of his house.

Such good social action, which nowadays we call social welfare, should always be promoted. The last two examples we cited are from the sunnah and the practice of the Prophet's companions. We find a very clear example in the Qur'an, as it relates the story of Moses when he arrived in Madyan after he left Egypt in his early adulthood. "When he arrived at the wells of Madyan, he found there a large group of people drawing water [for their herds and flocks], and at some distance from them he found two women who were keeping back their flock. He asked them: 'What is the matter with you two?' They said: 'We cannot water [our animals] until the herdsmen drive home. Our father is a very old man.' So he watered their flock for them, and then he withdrew into the shade and prayed: 'My Lord! Truly am I in dire need of any good which You may send me.'" (28: 23-24)

Let us reflect on Moses' attitude. He is a stranger in the foreign town of Madyan. A stranger is normally cautious in his behaviour, particularly when he approaches women from the town where he is a foreigner. However, he sees at some distance these 'two women keeping back their flock', while 'a large group of people were drawing water' for their herds and flocks. He immediately senses that there could be a case where a man's help would be handy. He does not hesitate to approach them. It is a strange situation that could involve some repercussions. He is a young man with undoubted strength, and they are two young women, but he is a stranger approaching them in the presence of a crowd of their townsfolk who were well aware of their situation and what they needed, but none was generous enough to offer help. Why would such a stranger address them in this way?

Here we find Moses motivated by his instinctive goodness. It does not matter whether help is needed by a man or a woman. He can provide such help, and so be it. It is the most natural thing in a society composed of men and women that they both should meet and exchange help and serve one another. Moses did not see any cause that should prevent him from asking: "What is the matter with you two?" Nor did the two young women find it embarrassing to talk to a stranger that was making his first appearance in their town. They succinctly stated their situation: "We cannot water [our animals] until the herdsmen drive home. Our father is a very old man." They did not hesitate to accept his help, as it was properly offered.

Then we see the two women's father sending one of them to call the stranger to come over and meet him. The man had helped his daughters and his conduct was without blemish, so the father needed to express his gratitude to him. The woman carried her father's message, walking shyly, which indicated that she was an honourable woman of high morality, unlike women who have suspicious motives for meeting men. Many life situations dictate that men and women should meet and exchange help for good purposes. This was such a meeting, starting with the help given to women who needed it and ending with an act of gratitude by the old father. It was a good meeting at every juncture.

All the examples we have cited involved good actions where the goodness is tangible. There are numerous other examples of action involving moral goodness, such as honouring people of distinction, congratulating others on their good occasions, visiting those who are ill, offering sympathy in a stressful situation and condolences at times of bereavement. All these are clearly encouraged by Islam. How can such noble feelings and sympathies be exchanged between men and women without their meeting together? Why should we deprive ourselves of such good feelings as if they were wrong, seeking to justify such restrictions as preventing temptation? Is it not enough to remind people that they must always remain God-fearing and warn them against yielding to temptation, allowing them at the same time to express their noble sentiments?

### 5. To Enjoin Right and Forbid Evil

Another advantage that stems from the social mixing of Muslim men and women is to implement the duty of enjoining what is right and forbidding what is wrong and unjust. God says in the Qur'an: "The believers, men and women, are friends to one another: They enjoin what is right and forbid what is wrong; they attend to their prayers, and pay their zakat, and obey God and His Messenger. It is on these that God will have mercy. Surely, God is Almighty, Wise." (9: 71)

This was indeed the standard practice of men and women in the early period of Islam. Anas ibn Mālik reports: "The Prophet passed by a woman weeping close to a grave. He said to her: 'Remain God-fearing and be patient in adversity.'" (Related by al-Bukhari and Muslim) Qays ibn Abi Ḥāzim reports: "Abu Bakr visited a woman from the tribe of Aḥmus called Zaynab bint al-Muhājir, but he found her silent, refusing to speak. He asked about the reason for her silence. He was told that she had set out on her hajj pledging to fulfil all duties of pilgrimage without speaking a word. He said to her: 'Speak normally. This vow of yours is unlawful because such vows go back to the days of ignorance.'"

Both of these examples show men giving advice to women. Conversely, can women undertake the same task and enjoin men to do what is right and proper?

Umm al-Dardā' and her husband were well known companions of the Prophet. We see her speaking to the Caliph without hesitation, enjoining him to maintain the proper behaviour Islam encourages. Zayd ibn Aslam narrated that 'Abd al-Malik ibn Marwan, the Caliph, sent a gift to Umm al-Dardā' consisting of some drapery and cushions. Sometime later, he woke up at night and called his servant. The servant might have been slow in his response, and 'Abd al-Malik cursed him. In the morning, Umm al-Dardā' said to the Caliph: "I overheard you cursing your servant when he was slow in responding to your call. I heard my husband Abu al-Dardā' quoting the Prophet's statement: 'Those who curse others shall not be accepted as intercessors or witnesses on the Day of Judgement.'" (Related by Muslim)

### 6. Participation in Jihad

Muslim women used to volunteer for jihad, considering it an honour which they were keen to have. Some of them joined several expeditions the Prophet led against different enemies. This continued up to, and including, his last expedition. It is pertinent to ask: could such female companions of the Prophet have joined those expeditions without meeting men and providing assistance to them? Indeed, women attended to different useful tasks on such expeditions. 'Umar said: "Umm Salīṭ well deserves to have a good garment. She carried heavy water containers for us during the Battle of Uhud." (Related by al-Bukhari) Umm 'Aṭiyyah said: "I joined God's Messenger on seven of his expeditions: I used to do guard duty in the camp and prepare food for the men." (Related by Muslim) Anas narrated: "When the Prophet went on an expedition, he would take Umm Sulaym and other Anṣārī women. They would attend to the injured." (Related by Muslim) Al-Rubayyi' bint Mu'awwidh said: "... We used to join the Prophet on his expeditions... and we would send the wounded and the dead back to Madinah." (Related by al-Bukhari)

One woman armed herself with a dagger to defend herself. Speaking of his mother, Anas reports: "Umm Sulaym had a dagger on the day of the Battle of Ḥunayn. The Prophet asked her about it, and she replied: 'I am arming myself with it so that if an unbeliever comes close to me, I will stab him in his belly.' The Prophet laughed." (Related by Muslim)

This was a case of self-defence in anticipation of such an eventuality. Another case of actual fighting by women was that of Umm 'Imārah who fought hard during the Battle of Uhud when things turned against the Muslim army. She fought defending the Prophet against the determined thrust of attack by the unbelievers who aimed to kill him. ʿUmar ibn al-Khaṭṭāb quotes the Prophet as saying on the day of the Battle of Uhud: "Whenever I turned right or left, I saw Umm ʿImārah fighting hard to defend me."

### 7. Professional Work

Another area where mixing between men and women is inevitable is the workplace. A woman may have to go out to work, either to help her husband in looking after their family, or to earn money which she may spend in what is beneficial and rewarding, or to discharge a collective duty of the community, such as teaching girls and women and treating them when they fall ill. It is often necessary for women who work for any such purpose to meet men and deal with them. Whatever work a woman may undertake, her commitments must not encroach on the rights of her husband and children. A woman is first and foremost responsible for looking after her home.

During the Prophet's time, many women took up jobs in different fields. Jābir reports: "The Prophet went to see Umm Mubashshir, a woman from the Anṣār, when she was on her date farm. He asked her whether the person who planted the date trees was a Muslim or an unbeliever. She replied that he was a Muslim. The Prophet commented: 'If a Muslim plants a tree or some other plants and a human being or an animal or another creature eats of it, what is eaten in this way counts as a *ṣadaqah*, or charity, he has given.'" (Related by Muslim)

Another case was that of the woman who worked as a shepherd. Saʿd ibn Muʿādh mentions that a slave woman belonging to Kaʿb ibn Mālik was tending sheep near Mount Salʿ when a sheep was badly injured. She caught the sheep and slaughtered it with a sharp stone. The Prophet was asked about the sheep and he said it was permissible to eat (Related by al-Bukhari). Other reported cases mention that another woman, Rufaydah, was a nurse, while some women worked from home in different ways. We include further texts speaking of women's professional work during the Prophet's time in Volume 3.

## 8. Political Activity

Moreover, Muslim women could be involved in political activity, in the broadest sense of the word. When people embrace Islam in defiance of opposition by their families, clans or the ruling authorities, they will inevitably be concerned about the welfare of Islam, and they may be subjected to pressures or persecution on account of accepting it. They may have to migrate from their country as a result. All this is part of political activity in our modern terminology. In the early days of Islam, Muslim women were involved in various such activities, motivated by their firm belief in the new faith and their willingness to defend it.

Texts mentioning aspects of women's involvement in political activity are included in Volume 3.

## 9. Facilitating Marriage

Some Qur'anic and hadith statements confirm that the provision of opportunities for men and women to meet in a healthy, clean environment where moral values are observed by all help to facilitate marriage. Here are some examples: the Qur'an mentions how the Prophet Moses (peace be upon him) married one of the two women he met as they attempted to water their sheep:

> When he arrived at the wells of Madyan, he found there a large group of people drawing water [for their herds and flocks], and at some distance from them he found two women who were keeping back their flock. He asked them: 'What is the matter with you two?' They said: 'We cannot water [our animals] until the herdsmen drive home. Our father is a very old man.' So he watered their flock for them, and then he withdrew into the shade and prayed:

> 'My Lord! Truly am I in dire need of any good which You may send me.' One of the two women then came back to him, walking shyly, and said: 'My father invites you, so that he might duly reward you for having watered our flock for us.' And when [Moses] went to him and told him his story, he said: 'Have no fear. You are now safe from those wrongdoing folk.' Said one of the two women: 'My father! Hire him; for the best person that you could hire is one who is strong and worthy of trust.' [The father] said: 'I will give you one of these two daughters of mine in marriage on the understanding that you will remain eight years in my service. If you should complete ten years, it will be of your own choice. I do not wish to impose any hardship on you. You will find me, if God so wills, an upright man.' Answered [Moses]: 'This is agreed between me and you.' (28: 23-28)

Another case is that of Prophet Muhammad himself when he proposed marriage to Juwayriyyah bint al-Ḥārith. Nāfi' narrated: "When the Prophet fought the tribe of al-Muṣṭalaq, he killed some of their men while their women and children were taken captive. He chose Juwayriyyah for himself [and married her]." (Related by al-Bukhari and Muslim) This case is reported differently by 'Ā'ishah, the Prophet's wife: "Juwayriyyah came to the Prophet seeking his help in buying her own freedom... The Prophet said to her: 'Would you consider a better offer?' She said: 'What offer, Messenger of God?' He said: 'I will pay for your freedom and marry you.' She said: 'I accept.'" (Related by Abu Dāwūd)

Another case from the Prophet's time is that of Subay'ah bint al-Ḥārith, who gave birth to a child soon after her husband's death. "When she completed her postnatal period, she began to wear make-up. Abu al-Sanābil ibn Ba'kak visited her and said: 'How is it that I see you adorning yourself, hoping to get married?'..." (Related by al-Bukhari and Muslim) Another version which is also related by al-Bukhari mentions that Abu al-Sanābil proposed to her but she refused him. A third version, related by Mālik, mentions that two men, a middle aged and a younger man proposed to her, but she preferred the younger man and married him.

From all these cases we realise that a Muslim man who wants to get married and can afford it does not do wrong if he looks at a woman carefully, trying to determine whether she would be a suitable wife for him. When he finds the right woman, he proceeds to make his proposal. This situation is different from that of a man who has already chosen the woman he wants to marry, either because he already knows her or on the basis of recommendation by others. He then goes to her family with a proposal, and the procedure is started. What we are talking about here is the case of someone intending to get married and searching for the right person. Thus, he looks around and tries to meet more than one woman, because he wants to be sure of the woman's personality, character, morality, family and upbringing, in addition to looking at her face and overall physical appearance. Needless to say, a man comes up with a proposal of marriage only when he is satisfied that he is making the right choice. What is important to emphasise here is that all this should be carried out only when a man is serious about getting married and with strict observation of Islamic standards of propriety.

Moreover, social mixing may encourage men who are not entertaining thoughts of marriage to give it serious thought. When a man who feels that he would rather delay taking upon himself the responsibilities associated with marriage meets and admires a certain woman, he may well change his mind. Furthermore, such mixing may remove obstacles to marriage placed by mistaken traditions. This was a clear phenomenon in the University of Khartoum in Sudan, where advocates of Islamic revival addressed their call to both male and female students. There were many cases of marriage between them. A similar situation took place in Egypt, when young members of the Islamic groups married. This was the result of a keen desire to adhere to Islamic teachings, maintain chastity and lead a clean and pure life. It would not have been possible without men and women meeting within the framework of Islamic activities at university.

What we are saying is that social mixing, within the limits Islam clearly defines, will produce good results, one of which is to make marriage easier for young people. We must emphasise the vital importance of observing Islamic rules in such social mixing, because going beyond them sets people on a slippery road that may lead to disastrous results.

### 10. Facilitating Relaxation, Attending Celebrations and Good Activities

There are certain types of occasions where women love to be fully relaxed, able to display their adornments, fine clothing, jewellery and make-up, and to sing and dance, etc. Islam does not prohibit such activities, but instead makes it clear that women should be on their own. They are not to mix with men on such occasions. This is an aspect of Islamic propriety.

There are, however, other types of social occasions which men and women can attend together, such as celebrating Eid. For such a celebration, a local community is encouraged to hold a function in an open space, to accommodate all people, men, women and children, including those who are unable to join the special Eid Prayer because they are menstruating. As they go out to attend the prayer, they repeat phrases of God's glorification in a joyful atmosphere. Similarly, if there is an event where some men perform some folklore dances, movements or plays, these are permissible for women to attend. Evidence for this is found in the case of 'Ā'ishah watching the Abyssinians as they performed their traditional play in the Prophet's mosque in his presence. On this basis, scholars agree that a woman may look at a man performing such activities, provided that there is no display of nakedness. The permissibility in this case is due to the difference in the conditions of men and women when they give such performances. Ibn Qudāmah, a Ḥanbalī scholar, said: "She may look at a man, except the part that must be covered." He cites 'Ā'ishah's watching the Abyssinians as evidence. Ibn Rushd said: "Men's looking at women is more serious than women's at men."

A different sort of fun activity which is attended by men and women together is in the supervision of children's play, both boys and girls.

In his *Ṣaḥīḥ* anthology of authentic hadiths, al-Bukhari gives us a full picture of how men and women participated together in celebrating the Eid during the Prophet's lifetime. This gives us a model for celebrating our happy occasions. We will include texts related to participation in celebrations and joyous events in Chapter 4 of this Volume.

## Conclusion

We have already discussed ten factors that encourage Muslim women's participation in social life and meeting men, based on solid evidence from the Qur'an and Hadith. The question is whether we should consider such mixed activity a sunnah, i.e. an action endorsed and recommended by the Prophet? The answer is that the evidence we have cited so far, and the far more numerous texts that we will be citing in the following chapters, confirm that such mixing is not merely lawful, but desirable and recommended, i.e. a sunnah or an approved Islamic tradition. This is based on the fact that such mixing was very frequent during the Prophet's lifetime and among his companions. It is, indeed, the practice he chose and implemented in all aspects of social life, making it part of the overall features of Islamic society during his lifetime. Moreover, it was indeed the practice of earlier prophets as we will see later on.

Some of our ancestors chose to segregate men and women, even though they acknowledged that integration and mixing is permissible. To us, however, the Prophet's practice is far more preferable and appealing than contrary practice, no matter who advocates it. It is his practice that we are ordered to follow, except where it is clearly indicated that a certain practice is applicable to him only. It is he who said: "The best guidance is Muhammad's."

Now that we have established that social mixing between men and women is a tradition approved of by the Prophet (peace be upon him), we need to establish whether this conclusion is based on certainty or probability. It is our confirmed view that around 300 pieces of text that include statements, actions and endorsements by the Prophet, all supporting the concept of social mixing, confirm that it is a sunnah based on certainty. The texts are clear, free of ambiguity, and the practice provides practical support, while the numbers ensure that the reporting is accurate and cannot be challenged.

The basis for such a certainty is discussed by Imam al-Shāṭibī who says: "The total evidence considered here is based on a number of pieces of evidence of the 'probable' level, all of which confirm the same point, thus elevating it to the level of certainty. Agreement makes the evidence more solid, and this is why multiple reporting, i.e. *tawātur*, implies certainty. This is one type of certainty. If looking at the evidence pertaining to a particular question provides a totality that gives certain knowledge, the required evidence thus becomes available. It is similar to implicit *tawātur*."

To sum up, God has given us a perfect method to follow. In one way, it is most suitable for honourable men and women, provided they abide by approved standards of propriety when they are together. In another, it is most suitable for an active and productive social life, when honourable men and women make the best of such proper mixing. Indeed this is characteristic of the Islamic way of life: it aims to ensure purity and propriety in social dealings while making things easy and profitable for people.

## New Social Trends Affecting Women's Participation

Our modern society has witnessed the emergence of new elements and situations that require greater mixing in order to fulfil the interests of both men and women. God sent His messengers with guidance which people should implement in their lives, bringing their practical lives in line with it, so as to make human life full of goodness. However, it is impossible to implement divine guidance without an accurate and thorough understanding of such guidance and a similarly accurate and discerning knowledge of society and its practices. The texts we already cited should give us an accurate picture of divine guidance on the question of social mixing. It is also important to formulate an enlightened view of modern society and its life. This should rely on the basis of field studies and surveys, rather than personal or preconceived ideas.

Scholars of later generations opted for a narrower and stricter view of social mixing, which is at variance with the practices during the Prophet's lifetime and during the early period of Islam. Nevertheless, these later scholars were aware of the social conditions that prevailed in their time to a better degree than what we see among present-day scholars. Hence, they approved different rulings for town and village women, ordering town women to cover their faces and stay at home. They considered that there was very limited need for women to go out. Most of their needs were fulfilled by slaves and servants. They had a more relaxed view in respect of village women who were not ordered to cover their faces or to stay at home. In villages, women went out every day to help their husbands, tend cattle, do the daily shopping, mixing with men in all these areas. What this meant was that a more relaxed type of life was needed in rural areas.

We need to fully understand that circumstances have changed considerably making city life much closer to village life of old, with regard to women's role. This is primarily true in respect of working women, but it also applies to housewives who need to do many duties in place of their husbands who are heavily involved in their own work. While this needs to be studied carefully, we can point out some new social practices that have a clear bearing on people's activities:

1. There has been an increased need for women to have jobs, in a wide variety of areas. This is needed by both society and the women themselves. It makes it imperative that women should go out to work where they meet men.
2. There is also a felt need in contemporary society for women to participate in social and political activities, which again leads to more mixing between the two sexes. A full discussion of this is included in Volume 3.
3. Modern society has become far more complex, with numerous institutions active in a variety of fields, such as education, medicine, different services, in addition to numerous government departments and offices. All these deal with individual men and women. With such a large number of institutions, there is increased need for women to go out in order to attend to their affairs and the affairs of their families. In the past, many of these institutions did not exist.
4. Domestic help is no longer available for most people in cities. This has led to an increased volume of women's daily duties at home and outside. A woman often finds herself required

to do things that bring her into contact with men, such as serving family guests, talking to tradesmen who come to do certain jobs, such as maintenance work for electrical appliances or services.

5. The complexity of modern life and long distances within the city makes it impractical for a man to attend to all the things which used to be expected of a head of a family in the past. For example, people these days often find it difficult to visit relatives. They can hardly attend to certain things such as meet school teachers to discuss their children's performance, take children to a doctor or hospital, or do the household shopping, etc. Such duties are often performed by women, increasing a housewife's burden and responsibilities and forcing her to go out and meet men.
6. In many cities, people mostly live in blocks of small flats, which see little sunshine and fresh air. This means that family outings are essential for relaxation.
7. In former days, people lived in large family homes which accommodated children who had grown up and married. Such extended families meant that there was less need to go and visit relatives living far away. This has now given way to a social set up based on small family units in large cities. Thus, if a woman wants to visit a close relative, which is highly recommended in Islam, she will need to use public transport.
8. Other features, such as smaller families, reduced contacts with neighbours, long distances between relatives, limited family friendships, migration lasting several years for better jobs, as well as better education opportunities in a wide variety of areas make it imperative for more social contact between men and women.

All these factors have led to a change in the way we approach marriage. In the past, relatives, neighbours and friends facilitated engagement and marriage. It is now necessary to find different ways of social introduction that leads to marriage. Much used to be done through the family, with the desire of marrying into another specific family which one knew and respected. The first quality of both parties was that they belonged to this or that family. Now that such ties have weakened, it is necessary to find other ways to help young people to choose their marriage partners. This can only be done through social mixing, in a serious environment, such as study, work or social and political activity. What we are speaking of here begins with casual contact through being in the same place on more than one occasion. This leads to an initial choice, before other steps are taken, such as gathering information about the other party from friends and relatives, before a formal engagement is made.

# CHAPTER II

## Values to Observe in Women's Participation in Social Life

CHAPTER SUMMARY:

- Essential factors that help to observe recognised values
- Values common to men and women
- Values applicable to women in particular
- What to do when certain values are ignored?

# *Values to Observe in Women's Participation in Social Life*

Islam defines certain values and manners which should be observed when men and women share and meet in social life. These provide a perfect framework that ensures a fine standard of propriety and morality, without interfering with the steady progress of the life of society. This framework promotes what is good and useful, steers away from what is bad, resists evil pressures and maintains good psychological health for both males and females as it prohibits all cheap arousal of the sexual urge. At the same time, it neither resorts to escape from reality nor creates excessive shyness or sensitivity when dealing with the other sex. It is a perfect framework of propriety. It imposes more restrictions on women in dress code, speech and movement, which causes some difficulty. Muslim women, however, bear this difficulty knowing that it does not stop them from attending to their needs, which may necessitate social mixing with men. Such needs may be numerous or few, according to circumstances in different communities and families. This, in turn, increases or decreases the degree of social mixing.

## Essential factors that help to observe the values of social participation.

The first of these is careful upbringing and education which seek to establish faith in the hearts of young people, facilitates attendance to worship and promotes good morality. Thus, young boys and girls grow up in an atmosphere that values purity and chastity and promotes a sense of responsibility in all. God says in the Qur'an: "Believers! Guard yourselves and your families against a Fire fuelled with people and stones." (66: 6) "Not one of all [the beings] that are in the heavens or on earth but shall appear before the Lord of Grace as a servant. Indeed, He has full cognisance of them. He has kept a strict count of their numbers, and, on the Day of Resurrection, every one of them will appear before Him all alone." (19: 93-95)

A large number of hadiths encourage kindness and proper upbringing of boys and girls, with greater emphasis on girls because they were often neglected and ill-treated in pre-Islamic societies. 'Ā'ishah quotes the Prophet as saying: "Anyone who is in a position of responsibility for young girls and is kind to them [should know that] they will provide him with protection from hell." (Related by al-Bukhari and Muslim) Needless to say, good upbringing and education is the highest and best form of kindness to young girls.

Abu Burdah narrated from his father that God's Messenger said: "Anyone who has a young slave girl and he gives her good education and upbringing, then sets her free and marries her will have a double reward." (Related by al-Bukhari) Such is the high value Islam places on educating and bringing up a slave girl. Needless to say, the reward attached to the upbringing of one's own daughter or relative is much higher.

Al-Rubayyi' bint Mu'awwidh, a companion of the Prophet, reports: "The Prophet sent heralds into the quarters of the Anṣār on the morning of 'Āshūrā', i.e. 10 Muharram, saying: 'Whoever started the day not fasting should fast the rest of the day, and whoever is fasting should continue his fast.' We observed fasting on that day ever since, and we made our young boys fast. We would make soft toys for them so that when any of them cried of hunger, we would give them the toy to distract them until the time when we ended the fast." (Related by al-Bukhari and Muslim)

The second factor is early marriage, which Islam encourages in order to help people maintain their chastity. A number of hadiths are clear in this respect. ʿAbdullāh ibn Masʿūd narrated that the Prophet said: "Young people, whoever of you can afford marriage, should get married, because marriage helps in lowering one's gaze [at women] and in maintaining chastity. Those who are unable to marry may fast, as fasting reduces desire." (Related by al-Bukhari and Muslim)

Two young men related to the Prophet went to him seeking help in getting married. When the Prophet listened to their request, he said to Maḥmiyah [a man who was in charge of the state's share of war gains], "Let this young man (al-Faḍl ibn al-ʿAbbās) marry your daughter," and he did so. He then said to Nawfal ibn al-Ḥārith, "And you give this young man [ʿAbd al-Muṭṭalib ibn Rabīʿah] your daughter to marry," and he did. He then said to Maḥmiyah: "Pay so much in dowry for them from the war gains." (Related by Muslim)

Fāṭimah bint Qays reports that the Prophet told her to marry Usāmah. "I married him, and God blessed our marriage and I was happy." (Related by Muslim) Usāmah was a young man when the Prophet made this proposal of marriage to Fāṭimah. According to some reports, he was not yet 16 at the time.[1]

---

1. People's ages are often miscalculated due to the fact that the Arabs did not define the year until ʿUmar started the lunar calendar. Usāmah was a young man certainly, but his participation in certain events during the Prophet's lifetime suggests that he was several years older. They calculated each year by the number of months, relying on the moon cycle, but they did not count years in order to establish dates.

While the forgoing hadiths encourage young men to get married, we have a hadith that encourages the marriage of young women. The Prophet says: "Had Usāmah been a girl, I would have adorned her and given her good appearance in order to get her married." (Related by Ibn Sa'd)

There is no doubt that marriage provides great help in maintaining morality, particularly when a man finds himself resisting temptation when meeting women. Moreover it helps men to lower their gaze. Jābir quotes the Prophet as saying: "If any of you admires a certain woman, and he fancies her, let him go to his wife and have sex with her. This will remove the thoughts that may trouble him." (Related by Muslim)

The third factor is to provide a limited room for mixing of adolescents under supervision. 'Abdullāh ibn 'Abbās narrated: "Al-Faḍl ['Abdullāh's brother] was riding behind the Prophet when a woman from Khath'am spoke to the Prophet. Al-Faḍl kept gazing at her and she looked at him. The Prophet kept turning al-Faḍl's face to the other direction..." (Related by al-Bukhari and Muslim) Another report by al-Ṭabarī quotes the Prophet's comments on the incident: "I saw a young man and a young woman, and I feared that Satan might come in between them."

Umm 'Aṭiyyah narrated: "We were ordered to go out on Eid Day, including virgin girls who were brought out of their seclusion." (Related by al-Bukhari) Another version of this hadith states: "The Prophet commanded us to bring out adolescent girls and those who were normally in seclusion." Ibn 'Abbās narrated that on the day when Makkah surrendered to the Prophet: "People came to the Prophet in large numbers, saying: 'Here is Muhammad. This is Muhammad.' Indeed, adolescent girls came out of their homes to see him." (Related by Muslim) These two hadiths confirm that Arabian traditions restricted the opportunities of young, adolescent women to go out such that they did not frequently meet young men. The Prophet appears here to have endorsed this tradition.

However, restricting meetings between adolescents from the two sexes does not mean that such meetings should be banned altogether. What we mean is that such meetings should be on a restricted scale and under proper supervision. Such supervision is provided by the family, so that meetings take place in the presence of a parent or relatives. If they meet outside the family, then others who are well respected by the adolescents concerned should be present. What is important to realise is that such meetings, in a safe environment, provide training in self-control for young people, boys and girls, and prepare them to conduct their future contacts within an atmosphere of propriety. Moreover, it is highly beneficial that young people are used to meeting the opposite sex on serious occasions within the family environment, observing Islamic standards of propriety. This acts as a safeguard against developing excessive shyness among religious young people, and curtails the enthusiasm of those who are driven by their desires, paying little heed for other considerations.

## Values common to men and women

Islam defines certain standards of propriety, some of which are gender specific while others are common to both sexes. One of the most important of this latter type is the need to ensure that any meeting between men and women should be a serious one. God instructs the Prophet's wives, and all Muslim women, saying: "Speak in an appropriate manner." (33: 32) This Qur'anic order makes clear that conversation between men and women must be within the limits of what is reasonable and appropriate. It must not include anything that Islam does not approve of. Hence, we said that any meeting between them must be serious, for what is serious between men and women is appropriate, while play and frivolity is inappropriate.

Having said that, we need to make clear that a word said in jest does not detract from the intended seriousness. An example is found in the following hadith, reported by Abu Mūsā al-Ash'arī: "Asmā' bint 'Umays visited Ḥafṣah, the Prophet's wife. Asmā' was one of those companions of the Prophet who had migrated to Abyssinia in the early years of Islam. 'Umar, [Ḥafṣah's father] entered while Asmā' was still with Ḥafṣah. When he saw her guest he asked Ḥafṣah who was her visitor. She said, 'Asmā' bint 'Umays.' 'Umar said: 'Is she the Abyssinian? Is she the seafarer?' Asmā' confirmed this. 'Umar said to her: 'We were ahead of you in migrating with the Prophet, and thus we have a better claim to him than you.' Feeling angry, she said: 'No way. By God, you were with God's Messenger and he fed the hungry ones and admonished the ones who were ignorant. We were in Abyssinia, the land of alien, hateful people, enduring that for the sake of God and His Messenger. By God, I shall taste neither food nor drink until I have mentioned what you said to God's Messenger (peace be upon him). We were hurt and scared, and I shall mention this to the Prophet and ask him. By God, I shall neither lie nor twist. I shall say no more than what has been said.'" (Related by al-Bukhari and Muslim)

Nor is it contrary to propriety that the conversation should include some friendly exchange. An example may be given here. Masrūq reports: "We went to visit 'Ā'ishah and found Ḥassān ibn Thābit with her, reciting his poetry which included some lines expressing love. Describing 'Ā'ishah as chaste, pure and wise who cannot be accused of anything unbecoming, and who does not engage in backbiting other women. 'Ā'ishah said to him: 'But you are not like that.'[2] Masrūq asked her: 'How come you permit him to visit you when

2. 'Ā'ishah's comment refers to the fact that when the False Story was circulated accusing her of adultery, Ḥassān was one of those who repeated it, and was subsequently punished for so doing. This was a sensitive issue with 'Ā'ishah. However, she pitied him as he grew blind in old age. It is said that he was over 100 years of age when he died.

God says: 'awesome suffering awaits the one who took on himself the lead among them.' (24: 11) She said: 'What suffering is greater than blindness?' She then added: 'He used to defend the Prophet against poets who abused him.'" (Related by al-Bukhari and Muslim)

It should be explained that Ḥassān ibn Thābit was one of the finest poets during the time of the Prophet. He had been a well-established poet before the advent of Islam. When Islam began to make headway in Madinah, Ḥassān embraced the new faith and used his poetic talent for the services of Islam. When poets from Makkah who were idolaters began to abuse Islam and the Prophet in their poetry, those Muslims in Madinah who were poets in their own right took upon themselves the task of defending the Prophet. Ḥassān was the most prominent among these. However, he made a serious slip when he was caught up with those who repeated the false accusation against 'Ā'ishah. Hence Masrūq's remark about her allowing him to visit her. But the point that supports our case in this report is the fact that Ḥassān was reciting poetry some of which was love poetry. None of those present took exception to this.

The second of these values is that which the Qur'an terms as 'lowering one's gaze.' The Qur'an instructs the Prophet in the following way: "Tell believing men to lower their gaze and to be mindful of their chastity. This is most conducive to their purity. God is certainly aware of all that they do. And tell believing women to lower their gaze and to be mindful of their chastity." (24: 30-31)

Scholars give clear explanation of what is meant by 'lowering one's gaze', highlighting a fine point in the Arabic expression that is very difficult to render into English. The requirement is to lower one's gaze a little, not to adopt an unnatural posture, such as looking at the ground all the time when one finds oneself in mixed company. However, a scholar like Ibn al-'Arabī explains that such 'lowering' means that people should not stare fixedly at members of the opposite sex, while 'Iyāḍ points out that to look at the parts of another person which Islam requires to be covered is forbidden, while lowering one's gaze when looking at other parts may be required in certain cases. Ibn 'Abd al-Barr mentions that looking innocently at a woman's face and hands is permissible for all, while a look that expresses how a man finds a woman attractive is forbidden, even though she is well dressed. Ibn Daqīq al-'Īd explains that the verse may be taken to refer to a situation where people may be infatuated with each other.

Al-Bukhari relates the hadith in which a pretty woman from the tribe of Khath'am stopped the Prophet to ask him about certain things. The Prophet had behind him on the same mount his young cousin al-Faḍl ibn al-'Abbās. The hadith mentions that al-Faḍl kept staring at the woman admiring her beauty and the Prophet stretched his hand from behind to turn al-Faḍl's face away from her. In his commentary on this hadith Ibn Ḥajar, the author of *Fatḥ al-Bārī*, quotes Ibn Baṭṭāl, an earlier scholar, who says: "The hadith indicates an order to lower one's gaze when strong attraction is feared. If this is not the case, the order does not apply. It also indicates that the Qur'anic instruction requires lowering one's gaze so as not to look at any part of a woman's body other than her face."

Ibn 'Abbās explains that minor sins are those indicated by the hadith in which Abu Hurayrah quotes the Prophet as saying: "God has assigned to every person his share of fornication which he is bound to have. The eye's fornication is through its gaze, while the tongue's is through speech. A person may wish and desire, but it is the genital that makes it all a reality or refrains from doing so." (Related by al-Bukhari and Muslim) This hadith shows clearly that what is forbidden is a gaze accompanied by desire, which means that an ordinary look that is not coupled with desire constitutes no sin.

Another hadith gives 'Ā'ishah's report of an event that took place in the Prophet's mosque. She says: "... it was a festive occasion when the Africans played with shields and spears. Either I asked the Prophet or he said to me, 'Would you like to watch?' I said: 'Yes.' He placed me behind him." In another version she adds: "He screened me with his robe." (Related by al-Bukhari and Muslim) Ibn Ḥajar, the author of a voluminous commentary on al-Bukhari's authentic anthology, the *Sahih*, says: "This addition indicates that the occasion took place after the order to the Prophet's wives to be screened was issued. The hadith indicates the permissibility of women's looking at men."

To sum up, social meeting between men and women entails that they look at each other. This is perfectly all right, as long as they behave decently, not gazing hard at each other or coupling their gaze with desire.

Another important aspect is to avoid hand-shaking between men and women at all times. If we are required to lower our gaze in the first place, avoiding touching each other is even more desirable, because physical contact is more likely to stir desire than a mere look. We have several hadiths that show the preference to avoid such physical contact, although they do not prohibit it when needed.

The first hadith shows that the Prophet did not shake hands with women when they pledged allegiance to him. 'Ā'ishah narrated: "The Prophet used to test women who migrated to Madinah with regard to their belief, in accordance with the terms of the relevant Qur'anic verse, 'Prophet, when believing women come to pledge their allegiance to you, that they would not associate any partners with God, and would not steal, commit adultery, kill their children, fabricate a falsehood between their hands and feet, or disobey you in anything right, then accept their pledge of allegiance, and pray to God to forgive them.' (60: 12) When a woman accepted these terms, the Prophet would say to her in words, 'I accept your pledge.' By God, never did the Prophet touch a woman's hand as he accepted her pledge of allegiance." (Related by al-Bukhari and Muslim)

On the other hand, we have hadiths that indicate the permissibility of physical contact when needed. Anas ibn Mālik reports: "Any slave woman in Madinah could come to the Prophet and take him by the hand anywhere she wanted." (Related by al-Bukhari) Ibn Ḥajar adds another version of this hadith related by Ahmad: "Any woman servant from Madinah could come to the Prophet and take God's Messenger by the hand. He would not take his hand out of hers. He would go with her wherever she wanted." (Also related by Ibn Mājah)

Al-Rubayyiʿ bint Muʿawwidh, a woman companion of the Prophet, said: "We, women, used to join the Prophet on jihad to give water to the fighters and serve them." In another version she says: "We used to attend to the wounded, and send them and the dead back to Madinah." (Related by al-Bukhari)

We can reconcile the different versions, one stating the Prophet's avoidance of shaking hands with women and the other allowing physical contact. The Prophet avoided shaking hands because it is a significant contact which would have become frequent, particularly in the Prophet's case as he always met men and women in large numbers. That would have created numerous occasions for shaking hands, as a greeting, or to request his prayers, or to pledge allegiance to him. This does not preclude other forms of physical contact which served to fulfil certain needs that were less frequent, or with certain women who were unlikely to stir any feelings. This means that in the first type of contact, i.e. giving the pledge of allegiance, the Prophet did not exclude the element of feelings in relation to women coming in large numbers to give him their pledges, and did not find a strong reason for shaking hands, while in the second there was clear need. From another point of view, the Prophet frequently met Umm Sulaym and her sister, Umm Ḥarām, the mother and aunt of Anas, his servant, respectively. In their cases, and some other ones, there was no suggestion of anything desirous.

In summing up, we say that the Prophet's avoidance of hand-shaking with women indicates that it is generally discouraged, but not forbidden. This discouragement was made by way of educating his community and closing the door that may lead to sin. Scholars agree that closing such doors is graded as desirable and preferable, not imperative. We think that we will be good followers of the Prophet's guidance if we try to generally avoid shaking hands and physical contact with the opposite sex, while conceding that it can be done in cases where it is unlikely to stir desire, provided that there is reasonable justification for it. This is the case when such hand-shaking is seen as a means of establishing trust or exchanging noble feelings between believers, as in the case of relatives and close friends, or on suitable occasions such as welcoming travellers on their return, or offering condolences, or encouraging good action.

In our present day society, where shaking hands between men and women is frequent when they meet, we may need to be a little flexible, particularly if this means avoiding causing embarrassment. Such flexibility may be needed, particularly when we consider that there is no clear statement prohibiting such contact.

The fourth value is to avoid congested areas, allowing men and women to move separately. Umm Salamah, the Prophet's wife, reports: "When God's Messenger finished his prayers with *salam*, the women would leave straightaway but he stayed a little while longer before he moved." (Related by al-Bukhari) Ibn Shihāb, an early scholar of high standing, comments: "I think that he stayed on to allow women to leave before those men who also wished to leave early caught up with them." This is, then, a matter of organisation when exiting the mosque. It is well known that exits at public places are often very congested at the end of a function. By staying on a few minutes, the Prophet allowed women to leave comfortably before men.

This is confirmed by the Prophet's suggestion to his companions: "Perhaps we should leave this door for women..." This was certainly to make their movement easier. On one occasion, the Prophet left the mosque and soon men and women were walking together in the middle of the road. The Prophet said to women: "Move to the side. It is not proper for you to walk in the middle. Keep to either side." Again, this was a simple measure to ensure that decency was maintained.

Similarly, congestion should be avoided in public places, but this does not mean that women should always be in the back, as is the case in the mosque. Keeping women to the back is a special case that applies to prayer only, whether prayer is performed in the mosque or at home, with strangers or with a husband and close relatives. On all occasions, other than prayers, Islamic values of propriety require separate seating and avoidance of congestion. This may be done by allocating a separate area within the meeting place for women, or by adopting any arrangement that ensures no overcrowding. What we are talking about here is that men and women should not be too close physically. It is in reference to this that Imam al-Sarakhsī, a leading Ḥanafī scholar, says: "A woman should not try to kiss the Black Stone [when doing the *ṭawāf* in the Ka'bah] if there are several people around it. She is required not to be too close to men and not to crowd with them. She kisses the Black Stone only if she finds the place clear."

A fifth important aspect of Islamic propriety is the prevention of one man being alone with one woman in an enclosed place. The Prophet says: "Let no man be alone with a woman unless she is accompanied by a *maḥram*, i.e. a close relative." (Related by al-Bukhari) Ibn Ḥajar, an authoritative commentator on hadith, says: "This indicates that being alone with a stranger woman is forbidden. This is unanimously agreed upon by scholars. However, they differ as to whether a *maḥram* can be replaced by others who ensure that the purpose is met, such as the presence of other reliable women. This is allowed because suspicion does not arise in such a scenario.

The following situations do not come under prohibited one-to-one meetings:

1. A meeting when other people are present. Under the heading 'permissibility of a man meeting a woman with people around', al-Bukhari relates: "Anas ibn Mālik reported that a woman from the Anṣār came to the Prophet and he met her alone. He said to her, 'By God, you, [the Anṣār], are the dearest people to me.'" (Related by al-Bukhari and Muslim) In commenting on this hadith Ibn Ḥajar says: "Such a one-to-one meeting should not be conducted in a way where they are physically unseen by others, or their conversation is unheard, as happens when a woman is saying something that she would be too shy to say in public." He also says that the hadith makes clear that speaking privately to a woman is not incompatible with Islam when both are safe from allurement.
2. A meeting of two or three men with one woman, when necessary. The supporting evidence is given in the hadith that quotes the Prophet as saying: "As from today, let not a man enter the home of a woman whose husband is absent, unless accompanied by one or two men." (Related by Muslim) Imam al-Nawawī, who wrote a commentary on Muslim's anthology of authentic hadiths, says: "At face value, this hadith allows two or three men to be alone with a woman unrelated to them, but scholars of our Shāfiʿī school agree that this is prohibited. Therefore, the hadith should be interpreted as meaning a group of honourable and God-fearing men who would never agree to indecency."

3. A meeting of one man with a group of women. The prohibited meeting is that of one man with one woman. When there are more men or women, the prohibition is removed. Al-Nawawī says: "Should a man visit a woman and he is alone with her, this is prohibited for both of them. If he visits a group of women unrelated to him, the majority of scholars agree that this is permissible. The evidence is clear in the hadith that says: 'As from today, let not a man enter the home of a woman whose husband is absent, unless accompanied by one or two men.' Moreover, when there is a group of women, a man cannot tempt one of them to join him in doing something indecent."

One of the values of propriety in Muslim society is that a man who wants to visit a married woman should have her husband's permission if the husband is in town. Abu Hurayrah quotes the Prophet as saying: "It is not permissible for a woman to fast [voluntarily] when her husband is present without his permission, nor is it permissible for her to admit a visitor into his home without his permission." (Related by al-Bukhari and Muslim) Another version reported by Muslim reads: "Nor is it permissible for her to admit a visitor into her husband's home when he is present without his permission."

In commenting on this hadith, Ibn Ḥajar discusses the condition of the husband's presence added in the second part as related by Muslim. He says that the husband's absence or his being away does not mean that a married woman can admit an individual man into his home. On the contrary, the prohibition is even clearer as we have authentic hadiths prohibiting a man visiting a woman when her husband is away, unless he is accompanied by others. The only way to understand this added condition is that when a husband is around, it is easy for the woman to obtain his permission first, while this is difficult when he is away.

The requirement of obtaining a husband's permission when he is around is further evidenced by the report that 'Amr ibn al-'Āṣ went to 'Alī ibn Abi Ṭālib's home for some business, but he did not find 'Alī at home. He left, then came again, two or three times, without finding him. When 'Alī came over, he said to 'Amr: "As you have some business with her, why did you not enter?" 'Amr said: "We have been prohibited from entering women's homes without their husbands' permission."

In a scenario where the husband is away, permission is not necessary, as indicated by a hadith we quoted earlier: "As from today, let not a man enter the home of a woman whose husband is absent, unless accompanied by one or two men."

Islamic propriety and decency also requires that long and repeated meetings between men and women should be avoided, as happens when frequent visits of relatives and friends last several hours, or when men and women meet all day long at the workplace, even though they are attending to their jobs.

Although these conditions are not included in any statement of the Qur'an or Hadith, they should nonetheless be observed. The point here is that when such repeated and long meetings become frequent, it becomes difficult to observe Islamic manners such as looking decently at the other person and maintaining seriousness in conversation and propriety of movement. These are required of both men and women when they meet. Therefore, and to implement the rule of closing doors leading to what is prohibited, it is advisable to refrain from such long and repeated meetings, unless the nature of one's job requires such frequent meetings, either for discussion or cooperation in completing certain tasks. In this case, there is no harm in meeting frequently, provided that people remain on their guard. Needless to say, people who are preoccupied with their jobs have no time for distractions, which in turn helps them to maintain propriety.

All this comes within the overall requirement that Muslims, men and women, should steer away from all indecency, committed publicly or privately. God says in the Qur'an: "Do not commit any shameful deed, whether open or secret." (6: 151) He also says: "Abstain from all sin, be it open or secret. Those who commit sins will be requited for what they have committed." (6: 120)

We have so far explained the standard of manners that both men and women should observe. A special requirement applied only to the Prophet's wives when they met men. Essentially, such meetings should be from behind a screen. God says in the Qur'an: "When you ask the Prophet's wives for something, do so from behind a screen." (33: 53) This screening applied only to the Prophet's wives. It merits special discussion and for which we will devote Chapter 2 of Volume 5.

## Values applicable to women

In addition, certain standards are required of women in particular. The first is that they should always wear clothes that fit with Islamic standards of decency. God says in the Qur'an: "Tell believing women... not to display their charms except what may ordinarily appear thereof. Let them draw their head-coverings over their bosoms." (24: 31) "Prophet! Say to your wives, daughters and all believing women that they should draw over themselves some of their outer garments." (33: 59) "Do not display your charms as they used to display them in the old days of pagan ignorance." (33: 33)

A number of hadiths speak about decency when women go out. Abu Hurayrah reports: "God's Messenger said: 'Two types of the dwellers of hell I did not see... The second is that of women whose clothing reveals much.'" (Related by Muslim) Umm 'Aṭiyyah mentions that she asked the Prophet when he ordered women to attend the Eid Prayer: "Is a woman excused from attending if she has no outer garment to wear?" He said: "Let her friend lend her an outer garment." (Related by al-Bukhari and Muslim) Fāṭimah bint Qays quotes the Prophet as saying to her: "I hate that your head covering should drop, or that your dress should be lifted to expose your legs and thus people would see of you what you would dislike them to see."

We will devote Volume 4 of this abridged series for a detailed discussion of the Islamic requirements of decent female attire, God willing.

Another important standard is to avoid wearing strong smelling perfume. Zaynab, ʻAbdullāh ibn Masʻūd's wife, reports: "God's Messenger told us: 'When any woman wants to come to the mosque, she should not wear perfume.'" (Related by Muslim) Abu *Mūsā* al-Ashʻar*ī* reports: "God's Messenger said: 'If a woman wears strong smelling perfume and she passes by a group of people who will sense her smell, then she is so-and-so.' His words were certainly very strong." (Related by Abu Dawood)

Other values Muslim women should observe include seriousness in speech and movement. God says in the Qur'an: "Do not speak too soft, lest any who is sick at heart should be moved with desire." (33: 32) "Let them not swing their legs in walking so as to draw attention to their hidden charms." (24: 31)

## When Islamic manners are ignored

Muslims, men and women, should always try to observe the qualities we have outlined whenever they meet. The question is what should they do when some of these qualities are ignored in a particular situation? The answer is that social corruption creeps in whenever these qualities are absent. In such a situation a Muslim feels uneasy. Therefore, he must weigh up the expected benefits against the likely loss. He should take part when the benefit is likely to be greater, and choose to have no part when loss is more likely. Every case should be considered on its own merits. However, the following points should be considered:

1. If avoiding mixing with the other sex in such circumstances might cause a Muslim some difficulty, either in relation to their work or the fulfilment of their interests or indeed in their overall affairs, then they must accept what is unavoidable, within the limits of what is necessary to remove such difficulty. God says in the Qur'an: "It is He Who has chosen you, and has laid no hardship on you in [anything that pertains to] religion." (22: 78)
2. Sometimes the participation of a Muslim in a function where Islamic requirements are absent will help to advance something good or prevent some evil. A Muslim may, for example, be able to enjoin what is good or prevent some evil action, or may impart useful knowledge to people who are unaware of it, or their mere presence may lead others to refrain from some actions that are unacceptable to Islam. In any such situation, the person concerned, man or woman, should participate. He or she should seek God's help and resolve to try to use such participation in order to achieve some good result. Their participation becomes even more required when violating Islamic moral standards is commonplace in society and such participation provides a good chance to point out the proper way to them.
3. By contrast, a Muslim must refrain from such participation if he or she fears that they may be tempted to do something forbidden. Likewise, if their absence causes the participants to review their conduct and refrain from what is sinful, then they must abstain from such functions.
4. Some Muslims may violate some aspects of Islamic values that should be observed when meeting with the opposite sex. This could be out of ignorance, or necessity or an unforeseen emergency, and the violation could take the form of a one-to-one meeting in an enclosed place. In such a case, Muslims must not suspect their brothers or sisters

of any wrongdoing. They should be careful not to criticise or accuse them, without evidence, in front of others. They should take warning from what happened in the event that God describes as 'the falsehood': "You took it up with your tongues and uttered with your mouths something of which you have no knowledge, thinking it a light matter whereas in God's sight it is grave indeed. If only when you heard it you said: 'It is not right for us to speak of this! All glory belongs to You. This is a monstrous slander.'" (24: 15-16) The Prophet says: "Sufficient it is of a sin that one should repeat to others all that one has heard."

5. A common practice that is akin to false accusation is to drop innuendoes about other people's motives and to accuse them on the basis of false reports, simply because some Muslims fall short of observing all Islamic manners. We are always required to take matters at face value, and to advise our fellow Muslims to observe the values God wants us all to observe. We must never judge others. Such judgement belongs to God alone.

Having said that, we must always remind ourselves and our brothers and sisters to always avoid putting ourselves in positions that invite gossip and evil thoughts.

# CHAPTER III

## When the Prophet's Wives Met Men in Public and Private

CHAPTER SUMMARY:

**Before the Obligation of Screening**

- Pursuit of knowledge
- When paying a visit
- Visiting the ill
- Seeking a ruling
- Receiving guests
- Enjoining what is right
- During military expeditions

**After the Obligation of Screening**

- Interested in what the Prophet discussed with people
- Accompanying the Prophet on journeys
- The Prophet shows his wife the Abyssinian dancing show
- Maintaining contacts with society
- Men visit them for various reasons
- Educating the Muslim community in the Prophet's sunnah

# *When the Prophet's Wives Met Men in Public and Private*

## Before the Obligation of Screening

It is well known that a divine order was given to the Prophet, late in his life, requiring his wives to be behind a screen when speaking to men. Prior to this order, they behaved like other Muslim women, taking part in the public life of society and meeting men on both public and private occasions. There are many examples of this on either very common occasions, such as the mere exchange of greetings, or special get-togethers such as weddings and parties. However, we will cite other examples so that we give an idea of the breadth of their participation in public life, and the variety of purposes of their meetings with men.

The first example concerns the pursuit of knowledge and goes back to Khadījah, the Prophet's first wife. 'Ā'ishah narrated: "The first aspect of revelation given to the Prophet was that his dreams would always come true... Khadījah took him to Waraqah ibn Nawfal, her cousin on her father's side. Waraqah had converted to Christianity prior to the advent of Islam. He used to write in Arabic whatever he learnt of the Gospel. He was an old, blind man. Khadījah said to him: 'Cousin! Listen to what your nephew [meaning Prophet Muhammad] has to tell you.' He said to him: 'Nephew! What is it you have seen?' The Prophet told him about his encounter with Gabriel, the angel. Waraqah said: 'This is the archangel who used to come to Moses. I wish I were a young man. I wish I am alive when your people will drive you out of your town.' The Prophet said: 'Will they drive me out?' Waraqah answered. 'Yes. No one has ever preached what you will be delivering without being met with hostility. If I am alive on that day, I will give you great support.'" (Related by al-Bukhari and Muslim)

After Khadījah's death, his first and only wife for 25 years, the Prophet married several wives who reported many of his statements and teachings. None more so than 'Ā'ishah, who was endowed with a rich wealth of knowledge. Sa'īd ibn al-'Āṣ reports that both 'Ā'ishah and 'Uthmān told him that Abu Bakr sought admission to speak to the Prophet when he was lying on his bed, wearing 'Ā'ishah's shawl. When Abu Bakr was admitted, the Prophet attended to his business, and then he left. Then 'Umar sought permission and he was admitted while the Prophet remained in the same position. When he finished his business, he left. 'Uthmān said: "I came later and sought permission. The Prophet sat up and told 'Ā'ishah to put her clothes together, covering herself well. I mentioned my business and the Prophet dealt with it. I then left." 'Ā'ishah said: "Messenger of God! How come you did not sit up and prepare yourself to receive either Abu Bakr or 'Umar as you did for 'Uthmān?" He said: "'Uthmān is a shy person. I feared that if I received him when I was in that position, he would not put his request to me." (Related by Muslim)

Usāmah ibn Zayd reports that "Gabriel, the angel came to the Prophet when he was at Umm Salamah's home, and he spoke to him before standing up and leaving. The Prophet asked his wife,

Umm Salamah, who that person was. She said: 'He is Diḥyah.' Umm Salamah said: 'By God, I had no doubt that the man was Diḥyah until I heard the Prophet speaking to the people, reporting what Gabriel said.'" (Related by al-Bukhari and Muslim)

It should perhaps be explained that sometimes Gabriel came to the Prophet taking the shape of a human being. On those occasions, he mostly appeared like Diḥyah ibn Khalīfah al-Kalbī, who was a very handsome companion of the Prophet. This explains how the Prophet's wife, Umm Salamah, thought Gabriel to be Diḥyah, but when she heard the Prophet addressing his companions and saying to them what Gabriel said earlier, she realized her mistake.

'Ā'ishah narrated: "A man asked the Prophet: 'If a man has intercourse with his wife and then feels too sleepy, do they have to take a bath?' As I was present the Prophet said to him: 'I do that myself with this one [pointing to me] and we take a bath later.'" (Related by Muslim)

'Ā'ishah narrated that when the Prophet's wives needed to go to the toilet they went at night to al-Manāṣiʿ, a wide, open place with no vegetation. ʿUmar used to say to the Prophet that he should keep his wives screened, but the Prophet did not do so. One night, Sawdah, one of the Prophet's wives, went out for that purpose. She was a tall woman. ʿUmar called out to her: "We have recognised you, Sawdah!" He did so out of his eagerness that the Prophet's wives should be screened. Soon afterwards God's order was revealed for them to be screened. (Related by al-Bukhari and Muslim)

Anas narrated: "On the day of the Battle of Uhud, fighters retreated, leaving the Prophet. I saw 'Ā'ishah bint Abu Bakr and Umm Sulaym, having lifted their skirts. I could see their anklets as they moved fast, carrying waterskins on their backs and pouring water in people's mouths before going back to fill up the waterskins and giving people to drink." (Related by al-Bukhari and Muslim)

Together these hadiths give us a picture of the Prophet's wives actively participating in the life of the Muslim community. When the Prophet was visited by some of his companions, they were often present, in case the Prophet needed anything. People put their cases, and asked for rulings, even on intimate matters such as intercourse between man and wife, when they might be present. The Prophet neither ordered them to go out, nor was he upset that the man should ask such a question while his wife was present. On the contrary, he answered him in a very relaxed manner, letting the question appear as very ordinary.

## After the Obligation of Screening

The Prophet's wives had special status, putting them in a class apart from all Muslim women, with special rules applying to them only. In the Qur'an, they were given the title 'Mothers of the Believers', yet all Muslim men were ordered not to speak to them unless they did so from behind a screen. Therefore, they were not to meet men in the way other Muslim women do, but were always to be screened from them. This applied for the rest of their lives, even though some of them lived for many years after the Prophet had passed away. All Muslims, throughout all generations up to the present day, have honoured them as their mothers. Yet the fact that they were to speak to people only from behind a screen did not prevent them from continuing their participation in the affairs of the Muslim community or speaking to men whenever the occasion arose. What the rules applicable to them meant was that certain manners needed to be observed when addressing or meeting them. Their participation in the social life of the community continued during the Prophet's lifetime and after he passed away.

### 1. Interested in what the Prophet said to people

When the Prophet went on an expedition, which might often involve a military confrontation or the threat of one, he took one of his wives with him, drawing lots among them to determine who came with him. After the Battle of Ḥunayn, in which the Muslims gained a very large amount of booty, the Prophet encamped at al-Jiʿirrānah, a place between Makkah and Madinah. Abu Mūsā al-Ashʿarī narrated: "I was with the Prophet together with Bilāl at that place when a Bedouin came to him and said: 'Are you not going to fulfil your promise to me?' The Prophet said: 'Soon enough! Rejoice.' The man said: 'You have given me too much of soon enough.' The Prophet moved towards me and Bilāl looking almost angry. He said to us: 'The man has refused the good news. Accept it, you two.' Both said: 'We do.' He asked for a jug of water, and washed his hands and face and rinsed his mouth. He then said to us: 'Drink of this water and wash your faces and necks, and rejoice at what will be coming soon.' We took the jug and did as he said. Umm Salamah called us from behind the screen saying: 'Keep some for your mother.' We kept some water for her." (Related by al-Bukhari and Muslim)

The relevant point to our discussion in this hadith is that Umm Salamah, the Prophet's wife, followed the conversation from behind a screen and took part in it, making her request directly to the two men, describing herself as their mother. Had social participation been denied to women, it would have been denied to the Prophet's wives, and Umm Salamah in this instance would have not spoken to the two men. She would have spoken only to her husband, the Prophet. This, however, was not the case. The Prophet did not object to her addressing them directly. Had it been objectionable, it would have been his duty to make that clear to all three, because his task was to deliver and explain God's message.

ʿĀ'ishah narrated: "A man sought permission to see the Prophet. The Prophet said: 'Admit him. An unpleasant person.' When he entered, the Prophet spoke to him kindly. [After he left] I said: 'Messenger of God, you said about the man what you said, then you spoke to him kindly!' He said: ''Ā'ishah, the worst of people are those people stay away from in order to avoid their evil doing.'" (Related by al-Bukhari and Muslim)

**2. Accompanying the Prophet on his journeys**

'Ā'ishah narrated: "When God's Messenger (peace be upon him) intended to go on a journey, he would draw lots between his wives. The one whose name is drawn would be accompanying the Prophet on that journey." (Related by al-Bukhari and Muslim)

**3. Maintaining contacts with society**

When the Prophet's wives were ordered to be screened, they continued to participate fully in the social and public affairs of their community. They considered their screening as a special ruling which they meticulously observed as it was expressly ordered by God in the Qur'an. They realized that they had a special position, providing a link between the Prophet in his private life at home and the Muslim community. Here are a few of the numerous examples of such participation.

At times, the Prophet wanted to speak to people so as to draw their attention to a particular point. He would call out to them to gather and he would then address them. Umm Salamah, one of his wives, reports: "I used to hear people speak about the Pool of the Hereafter but the Prophet did not mention it in my presence. One day I was at home, with my maid doing my hair, when I heard the Prophet calling on people to gather. I told the maid to stop. She said: 'He has called on only men to come to him, but he did not call the women.' I said: 'He called the people and I am one of the people.' The Prophet said in his address: 'I shall be ahead of you preparing things at the Pool. Let no one of you be turned away when he tries to come forward to me. I will ask why he is turned away and I will be told: You do not know what they perpetrated after you had gone.' I will then say: 'Away with them.'" (Related by Muslim)

The point here is that Umm Salamah was keen to attend a public address by the Prophet, considering herself one of the people. She could have stayed at home and learnt what the Prophet said to the people when he went to see her later that afternoon, as was his habit with all his wives, but she felt that she needed to be with the people, listening with them.

Another of the Prophet's wives, Zaynab bint Jaḥsh, was a model of generosity, taking care of the poor and helping those in need of any kind of help. Several reports confirm this quality. In fact she excelled in handicrafts, selling her artefacts and donating the proceeds to good causes. 'Ā'ishah narrated: "One or the other of the Prophet's wives asked him who of them would be the first to die after him. He said: 'The one with the longest hand.' They took a stick to measure their hands, and concluded that Sawdah [who was a tall woman] had the longest hand. However, when Zaynab was the first of them to die after the Prophet, they realized that the Prophet's expression, 'the longest hand', referred to the one who was the most charitable. Zaynab simply loved to give to charity." (Related by al-Bukhari and Muslim) In another hadith, 'Ā'ishah says: "... I have never seen a woman who is better in faith or more God-fearing or truthful in what she says or kind to relatives or charitable or more modest in her work through which she earns what she gives for charity, purely to please God, than Zaynab [bint Jaḥsh]." (Related by Muslim) Ibn Ḥajar quotes a hadith related by al-Ḥākim who collected an anthology of authentic hadiths fulfilling the criteria set by al-Bukhari and Muslim but missed out by both scholars. In this hadith 'Ā'ishah says: "Zaynab was clever in handicrafts: she used to tan and make leather articles, giving her profits to charity."

The Prophet's wives were ready to give advice whenever such was needed. While this advice was appreciated by the person who received it, it was also a special type of advice that could be given to the Prophet concerning a public affair. When the Prophet travelled with 1,400 of his companions, heading to Makkah to perform the *'umrah* when Makkah was still under the unbelievers' control, they were stopped by its people. Prolonged negotiations led to the al-Hudaybiyah peace agreement which stipulated that the Prophet and his companions would return to Madinah without entering Makkah, while they would be allowed to visit the Ka'bah and do the *'umrah* the following year, staying only three days. Since the Prophet and his companions were already in their state of consecration, or *iḥrām*, they needed to release themselves by slaughtering their sacrifice and shaving their heads, or cutting their hair short. The Prophet told them to do so, and repeated his orders three times. They felt very sad and despondent, because they had eagerly looked forward to this visit to the Ka'bah but now realized that it was not to be. None of them did as the Prophet told them.

Depressed at this lack of compliance, the Prophet went into his tent and complained to his wife, Umm Salamah, telling her that they could incur a grave sin. She gave him sound, practical advice, saying: "Messenger of God! Would you like this to be sorted out? Go out but do not speak to any of them until you have slaughtered your own sacrifice and got a man to shave your head." The Prophet did exactly that. When his companions saw what he had done, they all slaughtered their sacrifice and shaved one another's heads.

The Prophet's wives continued to be fully involved in the affairs of the Muslim community. A case in point is that of Umm Salamah and her expressed sympathy with Ka'b ibn Mālik during the difficult time he endured. Ka'b's son, 'Abdullāh, narrated: "I heard my father, Ka'b ibn Mālik, one of the three people whose repentance God has accepted, saying that he did not stay behind for any of the Prophet's military expeditions except Badr and the Tabuk Expedition. He said: 'I resolved in mid-morning to speak the truth to God's Messenger (peace be upon him). He mostly returned from his travels mid-morning. He would go first to the mosque and pray two *rak'ahs*... The

Prophet ordered that no one should speak to me or to my two fellows, but he did not order the same regarding anyone else of those who stayed behind. People stopped speaking to us. We remained in this situation and I felt it went on too long. Nothing was more worrying to me than that I could die and the Prophet would not offer the Funeral Prayer for me or that the Prophet died and I remained in this situation where no one spoke to me and no one would offer the Funeral Prayer for me. Then God revealed to the Prophet His acceptance of our repentance, and this was in the last third of a night when the Prophet was with Umm Salamah. She was kind to me and concerned about me. God's Messenger said to her: "Umm Salamah, Ka'b's repentance has been accepted." She said: "May I send to him the good news?" He said: "People will then crowd here and prevent you sleeping." When God's Messenger finished the Fajr Prayer, he informed the people of the acceptance of our repentance. When the Prophet received good news, his face brightened like a piece of the moon.'"

The Prophet's wives were keen to learn the situation of different Muslim communities even when they lived in faraway places. 'Abd al-Raḥmān ibn Shamāsah narrated: "I visited 'Ā'ishah to ask her about something. She said: 'Where do you come from?' I said: 'I am from Egypt.' She said: 'How did your leader treat you during this expedition of yours?' I said: 'We cannot fault him. Whoever of us lost a camel, he would give him a camel; and whoever lost a slave, he would give him a slave. If anyone needed money, he would give him.' She said: 'What he did to my brother, Muhammad ibn Abu Bakr, does not stop me telling you what I heard God's Messenger (peace be upon him) say in this home of mine. He said: "My Lord, whoever is in charge of some affairs of my community and he is hard to them, be hard to him; and whoever is in charge of some of their affairs and is kind to them, be kind to him."'" (Related by Muslim)

Involvement in community affairs could also be seen with regard to cases of individuals. Sa'd ibn Abi Waqqāṣ was one of the earliest companions of the Prophet, and a great servant of Islam. When he died, 'Ā'ishah instructed people to bring his coffin into the mosque so that she could offer the funeral, i.e. *Janāzah*, Prayer for the deceased. People thought that this was singular, as *Janāzah* Prayer was normally performed outside the mosque, shortly before burial. She commented: "How quickly people forget. The Prophet performed this prayer in the mosque when Suhayl ibn al-Bayḍā' died." (Related by Muslim)

**4. Men visit the Prophet's wives for various reasons**

A wonderful aspect of the life of the Prophet's wives is that they were often visited by the Prophet's companions despite the fact that they were ordered to always be behind a screen when they met men. Visits did take place during the Prophet's lifetime and more often after he had passed away, for a variety of purposes. An authentic hadith speaking of a time when the Prophet was still alive mentions that 'Umar visited three of the Prophet's wives in succession, asking about something that puzzled him.

'Umar ibn al-Khaṭṭāb reported: "I was deliberating over something when my wife said to me: 'If you would do this or that...' I said: "Why are you interfering in my affairs? Why do you interfere in something that does not concern you?" She said: "Amazing is your attitude, Ibn al-Khaṭṭāb! You do not want to be objected to when your daughter objects to the Prophet and he remains angry for the rest of the day!" 'Umar put on his clothes and went to see his daughter, Ḥafṣah... 'Umar said: "I then left her and went to Umm Salamah, who was related to me, and I spoke to her about this. She said to me: 'How amazing is your attitude, Ibn al-Khaṭṭāb! You have interfered in everything and now you want to interfere between the Prophet and his wives?' Her words affected me so strongly that I calmed a bit." (Related by al-Bukhari and Muslim)

Visits to the Prophet's wives could be social, having no particular purpose other than that: many reports mention such visits. Masrūq, who belonged to the *tābi'īn* generation that succeeded the Prophet's companions, narrated: "We visited 'Ā'ishah and found Ḥassān ibn Thābit at her place, reciting some of his poetry. In one line he described her as: 'Chaste, sagacious and above suspicion. She never indulges in gossip about other women.' 'Ā'ishah said to him: 'But you are unlike that.'" Masrūq said to her: "Why do you allow him to visit you when God said about the event in which he was involved, 'Awesome suffering awaits the one who took on himself the lead among them?'" She said: "What suffering is greater than blindness? Besides, he used his poetry to defend the Prophet." (Related by al-Bukhari and Muslim)

The Prophet's wives were also visited when they were ill. Visiting the ill to comfort and reassure them, and to tell them that we think of them and to sympathise with their troubles, is an important act of kindness that cements relations within society. It is a well-established social tradition in any Muslim community. It goes back to the days when the Prophet laid down the basis of the Islamic society. Abu Mulaykah narrated: "'Abdullāh ibn 'Abbās, the Prophet's cousin, sought permission to visit 'Ā'ishah when she was in her final illness. She said: 'I fear that he might praise me.' They said: 'He is the Prophet's cousin and a distinguished figure in the Muslim community.' She let him come in. He asked her how she felt. She said: 'I am in a good state if I remain God-fearing.' He said: 'You are in a good state. You are the Prophet's wife, and the only one who was a virgin among his wives. Your innocence was confirmed by God...'" In another version of this hadith, he is reported to have added: "Mother of the believers! You shall join those noble people who went ahead of you: God's Messenger and Abu Bakr." (Related by al-Bukhari)

### 5. Educating the Muslim community in the Prophet's sunnah

The Prophet's wives were a source of education for his companions and their successors. People went to them on all occasions to ask about the Prophet's practice in different areas. Anas ibn Mālik narrated: "Three men came to the Prophet's homes enquiring from his wives about his worship at home. When they were told the details, they appeared to think that it was less than what is adequate. They said to each other: 'Our position is far below that of the Prophet. He has been forgiven all his sins, past, present and future.' One of them said: 'I will pray all night every night for the rest of my life.' The second said: 'I will fast every day without fail.' The third said: 'As for me, I will never marry.' The Prophet went to them and said: 'Are you the ones who said so and so? By God, I am the most God-fearing person among you, yet I fast some days and do not fast on others, and I pray at night but I also sleep, and I do marry. Such is my tradition and anyone who does not follow my tradition does not belong to me.'" (Related by al-Bukhari and Muslim) We note here that men went to the Prophet's wives in his lifetime, enquiring about his voluntary worship.

We are told in the Qur'an that following the Prophet's practice in any matter pertaining to religion is strongly recommended and earns reward from God. 'Alqamah, a scholar of the *tābi'īn* generation, reports: "I said to 'Ā'ishah, 'Mother of the believers! Tell me about the Prophet's practice and whether he singled out certain days for particular voluntary worship.' She said: 'No. He used to offer his voluntary worship all the time. Who of you can do what the Prophet used to do?'" (Related by Muslim)

'Ubaydullāh ibn al-Qibṭiyyah narrated: "Al-Ḥārith ibn Abi Rabī'ah, 'Abdullāh ibn Ṣafwān and I visited Umm Salamah, the Mother of the Believers. They asked her about the army that would be swallowed by the earth. This was during Ibn al-Zubayr's time. She said: 'God's Messenger (peace be upon him) said, "Someone seeks shelter by the Ka'bah, and a host is sent to him. When they will be crossing a desert area, they will be swallowed by the earth." I said: "Messenger of God, how about the one who was forced to join them?" He said: "He will be swallowed like them, but on the Day of Judgement, he will be resurrected according to his own intention."'"

We conclude our discussion of how the Prophet's wives always remained interactive with the rest of the Muslim community despite having to be always behind a screen when men attended them, by citing a hadith that gives a more detailed picture of how people really kept in contact with them. ʻĀ'ishah bint Ṭalḥah reports: "I used to be at ʻĀ'ishah's home as she raised me and I was in her care. People used to come to her from all areas. Older men used to come to me because of my relation with her and younger men used to consider me as a sister, giving me gifts and sending me letters from every province. I would say to ʻĀ'ishah, 'Aunt! This letter has been sent by this man, and this is his gift.' She would say to me, 'Daughter! Answer him and send him a gift in return. If you do not have something to send him, I will give you.' She would give me something to send." (Related by al-Bukhari in *al-Adab al-Mufrad*)

Note: Some of these texts speaking of the Prophet's wives will be cited again when we discuss how women believers used to meet men in various life situations. The reason is that the same rulings that apply to Muslim women also apply to the Prophet's wives, except for what is specifically addressed to the Prophet's wives and does not apply to other women. They were the only ones required to speak to men from behind a screen, but this did not mean that they were required to be in total isolation from life around them. Hence, they continued to be in contact with people and society in general.

# CHAPTER IV

# *Muslim Women's Participation in Social Life during the Prophet's Lifetime*

## Foreword

We will include in this chapter numerous texts that are relevant to the theme of women's participation in social life during the Prophet's lifetime. We need, however, to mention the following observations about these texts.

1. There is hardly an aspect of public or private life where Muslim men and women did not participate and mix during the Prophet's lifetime.
2. Most of the texts we will be quoting speak of young or mature women, some of whom were indeed in the prime of life. They do not speak of elderly women of the type mentioned in the Qur'anic verse that says: "Such elderly women as are past the

prospect of marriage incur no sin if they lay aside their [outer] garments, provided they do not make a showy display of their charms. But it is better for them to be modest." (24: 60)

3. Some texts may be quoted more than once, because they may cover different aspects, providing evidence to support a conclusion in each aspect. A text is repeated as many times as the areas to which it pertains. We feel that it is better to repeat the text than to mention it once and then refer to it each time we feel it is relevant. At times, we repeat only the part that is relevant to the subject under discussion.
4. Taken in totality, these texts quoted from the Qur'an and the two hadith anthologies of al-Bukhari and Muslim, prove that serious mixing that observes Islamic standards of propriety was the common practice approved of by God's Messenger. We could not find a single text discouraging, even implicitly, social mixing that observes such propriety. We may add comments by some scholars endorsing the permissibility of mixing in all social situations. We have been selective in these, choosing only those which confirm the view that mixing in all areas and situations is by no means a recent view.
5. Most texts we quote indicate that meeting between Muslim men and women was intended, and a matter of choice by both parties. Few texts speak of unintended meetings, and few others speak of meetings between Muslim men and non-Muslim women. We quote these in order to give a complete picture of social life in the early Islamic society established by the Prophet.
6. The texts we will be quoting vary widely. Some are definitive or very clear in their import while others may be subject to debate. We rely on the first type when stating a ruling. Some relate to events that took place prior to the revelation of the verse requiring the Prophet's wives to remain behind a screen. Others relate to events after its revelation. Neither case is relevant to the import of the texts because the screening

requirement applies only to the Prophet's wives and no one else. Some texts are peculiar to the Prophet's wives, while others are universal in their applicability. Some texts relate to a meeting with the Prophet alone, or in the presence of one or more of his companions, while others refer to a meeting with one or more of the Prophet's companions without his presence. Some mention a meeting of one woman with one man or more, and others mention a group of women meeting a man or several men. Some refer to a short, casual meeting while others to long and frequent meetings.

Because the duration and place of meeting are of much importance, we point out four different levels of meeting:

- A casual short meeting at home to attend to immediate business, such as a specific request, consultation or request for a ruling, asking for help, a prayer, presenting a gift, visiting a sick person, offering condolences, etc.
- A casual short meeting in public, such as taking part in functions in the mosque, requesting a ruling on a specific case, offering advice, litigation, and speaking to those in authority.
- A long or frequent meeting at home, such as when paying a visit, offering hospitality, providing accommodation, or giving home help.
- A long or frequent meeting in public, such as participation in jihad, meetings during travel, taking part in social occasions or in some professional business.

## Exchange of greeting

We begin with two hadiths mentioning an exchange of greetings between men and women. Sahl, a companion of the Prophet, reported that some of the Prophet's companions had something to look forward to on Fridays. When asked what that was, he said: "One of our elderly women used to send someone to the Buḍāʿah farm to bring her stems of some plants which she would put in a saucepan and add ground barley and cook them. When we finished our Friday Prayer, we would greet her. She served us of her cooking and we were delighted with it. We had had neither a nap nor eaten lunch before Friday Prayer." (Related by al-Bukhari)

ʿĀ'ishah narrated: "The Prophet once told me: 'Here is Gabriel extending greetings to you.' I said: 'And peace be to him, together with God's grace and blessings. You, Prophet, see what we cannot see.'" (Related by al-Bukhari and Muslim)

It should be pointed out that al-Bukhari enters these two hadiths under the heading, 'Greetings exchanged between men and women.' Ibn Ḥajar points out that by entering these hadiths under this heading, al-Bukhari refutes the import of a hadith related by ʿAbd al-Razzāq which states: "It is reprehensible that men should extend greetings to women, or women to men." This hadith is very poor in authenticity. The two hadiths entered by al-Bukhari indicate that this is perfectly permissible. Another authentic hadith which does not meet al-Bukhari's criteria is related by al-Tirmidhī on the authority of Asmā' bint Yazīd: "The Prophet passed by us, a group of women, and greeted us." As this hadith does not fulfil al-Bukhari's conditions of authentic hadiths, he only cited what meets his conditions. However, it is endorsed by a hadith narrated by Jābir and related by Ahmad. Further, Abu Nuʿaym includes under the heading, 'Action of a Day and a Night', a hadith narrated by Wāthilah attributing to the Prophet the statement: "Men may greet women, but women may not greet men," but its chain of transmission is very poor.

An authentic hadith related by Muslim quotes Umm Hāni', the Prophet's cousin: "I went to the Prophet and found him taking a bath. I greeted him..."

Commenting on the hadith quoting the Prophet as saying: "'Ā'ishah, here is Gabriel extending greetings to you," Ibn al-Tīn mentions that al-Dāwūdī objects by saying: "Angels are not referred to as men, but God refers to them in the masculine form." In answer we may say that Gabriel used to come to the Prophet in the shape of a man. Ibn Baṭṭāl quotes al-Muhallab who says that greetings between men and women is permissible, if no temptation is feared. Mālikī scholars differentiate between young and elderly women as a safeguard. Al-Muhallab said: "Mālik's argument is based on the hadith narrated by Sahl. The men they visited and who gave them food were not related to her. Therefore, if there are men and women at a place, greeting by either side is permissible, if no temptation is feared."

## Mixing in the Mosque

The mosque is the most important institution in Islamic society. It is the centre of worship, education as well as social and political activity. It is also the place where public meetings take place, and it provides a sports arena when necessary. Therefore, during the Prophet's lifetime, women were welcome in the mosque whenever they wished to go there. As women frequented the Prophet's mosque, they were able to directly participate in public life, in addition to taking part in worship, listening to the Qur'an as it was recited in prayer, attending lectures and classes and taking interest in the Muslim community's social or political concerns. Moreover, women met in the mosque and were, thus, able to strengthen their ties of friendship. What this means is that during the Prophet's lifetime, the mosque was a very active centre bustling with worship, cultural and social activities for men and women alike. Therefore, no one can deprive women of their right to frequent the mosque. To force women to pray at home, claiming that this is preferable, constitutes a sinful practice, since it means disobeying the Prophet who ordered us not to prevent women from attending the mosque. When a woman goes to the mosque for worship, or to listen to words of wisdom, attend a public activity, meet other Muslim women to strengthen ties with them, or to help in some good thing, then that benefit will be hers. Her good action may be obligatory or recommended. The Prophet says: "Whoever comes to the mosque for a particular purpose will have the benefit of that purpose."

The Prophet says: "Prayer offered in congregation in the mosque is rewarded 25 times more than the same prayer offered at home or in the market place." Commenting on the hadith, Ibn Daqīq al-'Īd says: "When a person performs ablution well at home and goes out to the mosque, for no purpose other than offering prayer, for every step he makes he is given a credit and one of his sins is erased. When he prays, the angels will pray for him throughout his prayer, saying, 'Our Lord, bless him, forgive him and bestow mercy on him.' While waiting for the prayer to be called, he is deemed to be in prayer... We need to look at the qualities mentioned in the hadith to be sure of its applicability. Although the hadith speaks of a man going to the mosque, since women are also encouraged to go to the mosque, then the hadith applies equally to them. No sex discrimination is valid with regard to the reward attached to good actions."

During the Prophet's lifetime, women not only attended the Prophet's mosque, but also attended mosques in other quarters and outside Madinah, as clearly appears from the following hadiths:

'Abdullāh ibn 'Umar narrated: "When people were offering the Fajr Prayer at the Qubā' Mosque, someone told them, 'The Prophet received Qur'anic revelations tonight commanding him to face the Ka'bah in Makkah. So, turn towards it.' They were facing Jerusalem, and therefore, they turned and faced Makkah." (Related by al-Bukhari) In his commentary on this hadith, Ibn Ḥajar writes: "The way this took place is explained in a hadith narrated by Thuwaylah bint Aslam in which she says, 'Women moved to take the place of men and men moved into the women's place. We offered the two remaining prostrations facing the Sacred Mosque in Makkah.'"

The Prophet emphasised women's right to attend the mosque, making it absolutely clear so as to allow no one to deprive them of this right. 'Abdullāh ibn 'Umar quotes the Prophet: "If your women request of you that they leave at night to attend the mosque, grant them their request." (Related by al-Bukhari and Muslim)

'Abdullāh ibn 'Umar reports: "A wife of 'Umar used to attend the Fajr and 'Ishā' Prayers with the congregation in the mosque. People said to her: 'Why do you go out at night when you know that 'Umar does not like that?' She said: 'What prevents him from stopping me?' They said: 'The fact that the Prophet ordered not to prevent women from attending mosques.'" (Related by al-Bukhari)

'Umar's dislike of his wife's action was merely his personal feeling. He did not like her to go out at night, even though she was only going to the mosque. People expected her to comply with his wishes, particularly because he was also the Caliph, or in modern parlance, the head of state. Hence they spoke to her. She said, he could easily order her not to go and she would comply. Her answer was meant as a reminder that she was only exercising her right which was sanctioned by the Prophet. It was 'Umar's awareness of the fact that he could not take up the issue with his wife.

Women's right to attend the mosque continued to be fully respected even after a woman was raped when she was walking towards the mosque to attend Fajr Prayer.

Since the mosque was, as we have described, a very active centre bustling with worship, cultural and social activities, women naturally attended it for no less than 12 different purposes, some of which were recommended, and some obligatory. The first of these purposes was offering obligatory prayers.

**First: For prayer** – Attending Fajr Prayer: 'Ā'ishah narrated: "Women believers used to attend Fajr Prayer with the Prophet, covering themselves with their shawls. They would return home when the prayer was over. They could not be recognized because of the darkness." (Related by al-Bukhari and Muslim) Ibn Ḥajar explains that the reference in this report is to leading figures among the Muslim women.

Attending Maghrib Prayer: Ibn 'Abbās narrated that his mother said to him after hearing him reciting Surah 77, *al-Mursalāt*: "Son, your recitation has reminded me that it was the last I heard the Prophet reciting and that was in Maghrib Prayer." Another version of this hadith adds: "He did not lead us in prayer after that until he passed away." (Related by al-Bukhari and Muslim)

And 'Ishā': 'Ā'ishah narrated: "One night the Prophet was late for 'Ishā' Prayer, until 'Umar called out to him saying: 'Women and children are overcome by sleep.' The Prophet went to the mosque to lead the prayer. He said: 'No one on the face of the earth is waiting for this prayer other than you.' At the time, Madinah was the only place where people prayed. They used to offer this prayer between the disappearance of the bright horizon and the end of the first third of the night." (Related by al-Bukhari and Muslim)

Friday Prayer: God says: "When people see some trade or entertainment, they head off towards it, leaving you standing there. Say: 'That which is with God is far better than any entertainment or trade. God is the best of providers.'" (62: 11)

Jābir ibn 'Abdullāh narrated: "We were with the Prophet attending a Friday Prayer when a caravan laden with food arrived. People went to it and only 12 people were left with the Prophet. God then revealed the verse that says: 'When people see some trade or entertainment, they head off towards it, leaving you standing there.'" (Related by al-Bukhari and Muslim) Ibn Ḥajar said that a report is mentioned in al-Ṭabarī's commentary and by Ibn Abi Ḥātim, with an authentic chain of transmission quoting Qatādah: "The Prophet asked the ones who remained how many they were. They counted themselves and comprised 12 men and women." Shaykh Nāṣir al-Dīn al-Albānī said that the authentic chain of transmission is up to Qatādah ibn Di'āmah, of the *tābi'īn*, not to Abu Qatādah who was a companion of the Prophet. As such, the hadith is classified as *mursal*, i.e. with an incomplete chain.

'Amrah bint 'Abd al-Raḥmān quotes her sister as saying: "I learnt the surah starting with '*Qāf*. By the glorious Qur'an, from the Prophet as he used to read it on the platform every Friday." (Related by Muslim)

These are obligatory prayers, but women also went to the mosque for voluntary, recommended and other prayers, as clearly evidenced by the following examples:

Anas ibn Mālik narrated: "The Prophet came once into the mosque and saw a rope tied between two pillars. He asked why the rope was put there. People told him: 'It is for Zaynab. When she feels drowsy, she holds on to it.' The Prophet said: 'This is not good. Remove it. One should pray only when one is fully alert. If one is tired then one should sit down.'" (Related by al-Bukhari and Muslim) Ibn Ḥajar points out that the hadith indicates that it is permissible for women to offer voluntary prayers in the mosque. Had this been not permissible, the Prophet would have made that clear. Ibn Ḥajar also adds that 'Umar organised night worship during Ramadan, appointing Ubay ibn Ka'b to lead the prayer. Ubay used to lead the men's congregation, while Tamīm al-Dārī led the women's congregation. That women needed a different imam was perhaps because they could not hear Ubay's recitation clearly. Therefore, they needed the one who led them in prayer to stand near them.

‘Ā’ishah narrated: “When Sa‘d ibn Abi Waqqāṣ died, the Prophet’s wives sent a word requesting that his coffin should be brought into the mosque so that they could offer the *Janāzah* , or Funeral Prayer for him. When the coffin was brought in, they stood near their rooms offering this prayer for him.” (Related by Muslim) Needless to say, their *Janāzah* Prayer was only voluntary, but the Prophet’s wives were keen to give it because they knew that Sa‘d was very close to the Prophet and related to him on his mother’s side.

Another voluntary prayer in which women participated in the mosque was the one offered at the time of a solar eclipse. Asmā’ bint Abu Bakr narrated: “I went into ‘Ā’ishah’s home when people were in prayer and I asked her why people were in prayer. [Apparently the time did not require a congregational prayer, and yet ‘Ā’ishah was praying with the congregation.] ‘Ā’ishah lifted her head to point to the sky and the sun’s eclipse. I said: ‘Is this a sign of God?’ She replied with a move of her head affirming such. The Prophet made the prayer very long and I almost fainted.” In Muslim’s version she adds: “It was an extremely hot day, yet the Prophet prolonged the prayer and some people fell down. I had a water skin close to me, and I opened it and poured some water over my head.” Muslim’s version adds further details quoting Asmā’: “The Prophet stood up too long and I felt like sitting down. However, I looked at a woman who was apparently weak and thought that she was weaker than me and I kept standing. The Prophet then bowed and made this movement too long. He then rose up again and was standing for a long while. Anyone who might have come at this point would have thought that the Prophet had not bowed yet. The Prophet finished his prayer when the eclipse was over and the sun appeared fully in the sky. He started to give a speech, beginning by praising God and glorifying Him. However, some women were talking to each other and I turned to them to ask them to keep quiet...” (Related by al-Bukhari and Muslim)

Al-Bukhari enters another version of this hadith under the heading: ‘Women pray with men during solar eclipse.’ Ibn Ḥajar points out that by doing so, al-Bukhari refutes the argument of scholars who prevent this, requiring women to offer this prayer individually.

Thus we see that women frequented the mosque for obligatory and voluntary prayers of all types. There was no restriction whatsoever on them doing so.

**Second:** ***i'tikāf*** – women went to the mosque during the Prophet's lifetime to perform the recommended practice of *i'tikāf*, which is to stay in the mosque up to ten days, engaged in all types of worship, including prayer, reciting the Qur'an, glorifying God and praising Him.

'Ā'ishah narrated: "The Prophet used to spend the last ten days of Ramadan in *i'tikāf* until he passed away. His wives used to do the same after that." (Related by al-Bukhari and Muslim) Ibn Daqīq al-'Īd explains that this hadith clearly indicates that this practice applies to men and women in the same way.

'Ā'ishah narrated: "I might occasionally enter my home during my time of *i'tikāf* only for a particular purpose. A sick person might be there, but I would only enquire after that person while passing by. The Prophet did not enter his home during his time of *i'tikāf* except for an urgent purpose." (Related by Muslim)

Another report by 'Ā'ishah indicates that a woman may also join in *i'tikāf* when she has a blood discharge other than her normal period: "One of the Prophet's wives joined him in *i'tikāf* while she was discharging blood, and she used to see red and yellow discharges. We might at times put a bowl between her legs when she was praying." (Related by al-Bukhari) Needless to say that the bowl was used so that the discharge did not fall on the floor of the mosque.

To explain the rulings about women's *i'tikāf* in the mosque, we quote the following dialogue from *al-Mudawwanah*, which is the most important work in the Mālikī school of *Fiqh*. The author is asking Ibn al-Qāsim, a leading authority:

Q. What does Mālik say concerning women's *i'tikāf* in the main mosque?
A. This is perfectly appropriate.

Q. Does Mālik require her to do the *i'tikāf* in her place of prayer at home?
A. No, this is not appropriate. The *i'tikāf* should be performed in mosques dedicated for God's worship.

Q. Suppose that a man permits his wife or slave, man or woman, to do the *i'tikāf*, but after they have started he wants to interrupt this, calling them back. Can he do so?
A. No, he cannot do so.

Q. Is this a ruling by Mālik?
A. Yes, it is his ruling.

We conclude this discussion by quoting a ruling by Imam Ibn al-Qayyim: "If a woman starts her period while she is in *i'tikāf*, her *i'tikāf* is not invalidated. She continues with it in the uncovered area of the mosque."

**The third purpose for which women went to the mosque during the Prophet's lifetime was to listen to what was being taught there.** Fāṭimah bint Qays narrated: "I went out to the mosque and joined the Prophet in prayer. When he had finished his prayer, he sat on the platform smiling." In another version she gives a report of what the Prophet said, starting with: "I have been told by Tamīm al-Dārī that a number of his tribesmen were in a boat when it broke up. Some of them were able to sit on a board from the wreckage and managed to reach an island..." (Related by Muslim) The Prophet was clearly using this story to give some of his teachings, and women joined in just like men.

**Fourth, women might also go to the mosque in order to visit someone during their period of *i'tikāf*.** Ṣafiyyah, the Prophet's wife, visited him in the mosque during his *i'tikāf* during the last ten days of Ramadan. She spent an hour talking to him before she rose to go home. The Prophet went with her, intentionally taking her home. When she was at the door of the mosque, near Umm Salamah's home, two men from the Anṣār passed by and greeted the Prophet. The Prophet said to them: "Stop a moment. This is Ṣafiyyah bint Ḥuyay." They said: "Messenger of God! All glory be to Him." They felt extremely uneasy [because the Prophet felt that he needed to explain that the woman with him was his wife]. The Prophet said to them, "Satan could be as close to a man as the blood in his veins. I feared that he might whisper something to you." (Related by al-Bukhari and Muslim) Both Ibn Ḥajar and Ibn Daqīq al-'Īd comment that this hadith proves that a woman may visit a man during his *i'tikāf*, and that it is permissible for a man doing *i'tikāf* to be alone with his wife in the mosque.

**Fifth: women also visited the mosque to pass time or to be in company with other women**. In other words, this was a social visit. Al-Rubayyi' bint Mu'awwidh narrated: "During the morning on 10 al-Muharram, the Prophet sent messengers to the quarters of the Anṣār, saying that whoever started the day fasting should continue his fast, and whoever did not was to fast the rest of the day. We used to fast on that day in subsequent years. We also made our children fast. We might make them a woollen doll." (Related by al-Bukhari and Muslim) In Muslim's version, she adds: "We would then go to the mosque... If children asked for food, we would give them the dolls to distract them so that they would be able to finish their fast."

A report in Ibn Sa'd's *al-Ṭabaqāt al-Kubrā* attributed to Khawlah bint Qays quotes her as saying: "During the Prophet's lifetime and Abu Bakr's reign, as well as the early years of 'Umar's reign, we, a group of women, would go to the mosque. We might take our knitting, and some of us might work with dry palm leaves. Then 'Umar said: 'I am going to stop you.'... He stopped us doing so, but we continued to attend the congregational prayers on time."

**Sixth: responding to a call to attend a public meeting. Fāṭimah bint Qays reports:** "... After I had finished my waiting period, I heard a crier carrying out the Prophet's instructions and calling people to assemble for prayer. I went with the people to attend. I was in the first line of women, which is the one next to the last line of men." (Related by Muslim) Imam Ibn al-Qayyim explains: "That the people of Madinah reported this is the same as their report of the Prophet's approval of women going out, walking along the roads, attending mosques and listening to speeches for which people are summoned."

**Seventh: another purpose was attending celebrations or social occasions.** 'Ā'ishah narrated: "God's Messenger was sitting close to my door when the Abyssinians were playing in the mosque. The Prophet covered me with his robe while I was watching their play." (Related by al-Bukhari and Muslim) Ibn Ḥajar quotes al-Muhallab's argument in reply to people who disapprove of playing in the mosque: "The mosque is a place to ensure the welfare of the Muslim community. Whatever is conducive to the benefit of the faith and the faithful is permissible to do in the mosque."

We have so far cited evidence in support of seven purposes for which women frequented the mosque during the Prophet's lifetime. **A different purpose is that a woman might also go to the mosque to offer herself in marriage to a God-fearing man**. Sahl ibn Sa'd reports that a woman came to the Prophet and said: "Messenger of God! I have come to make of myself a present to you." The Prophet looked up and down at her several times, then he lowered his head. When the woman realized that the Prophet did not make a decision concerning her offer, she sat down. (Related by al-Bukhari and Muslim) Ibn Ḥajar adds that a different version of this hadith quoted by Sufyan al-Thawrī specifies that this occurred in the mosque.

**The ninth purpose is to attend a court or a tribunal looking into a case**. Sahl ibn Sa'd reports: "A man said to the Prophet: 'Messenger of God! If a man finds his wife with another man, could he kill him?...' Then the man and his wife exchanged oaths in the mosque when I was a witness." (Related by al-Bukhari and Muslim) The oaths here refer to the requirement of the man accusing his wife of adultery to swear five times that his accusation is true. She can refute the accusation by swearing five times that he is lying. This causes the annulment of their marriage, but neither is punished as the case cannot be proven.

**Purpose number ten is to attend to the sick and injured**. 'Ā'ishah narrated: "Sa'd ibn Mu'ādh was injured, receiving a cut in a main vein in his arm, during the encounter of the Moat. The Prophet ordered that a tent should be erected for him in the mosque so that he could easily visit him. People were surprised one night when they saw blood coming through underneath the tent. They shouted: 'You people in the tent! What is this coming out from your side?' They found out that Sa'd was bleeding again. He continued to bleed until he died." (Related by al-Bukhari)

Other reports explain that Rufaydah of the Aslam tribe used to attend the injured in battle. The Prophet ordered the tent to be erected for Sa'd where Rufaydah was nursing him. The Prophet said: "Put him in her tent so that I can visit him every now and then."

**Cleaning the mosque was another purpose for women to visit the mosque**. Abu Hurayrah narrated: "A black man or a black woman used to sweep the floor of the mosque, but then that person died. [Al-Bukhari adds in another version, 'most probably the person was a woman'.] The Prophet missed that person and on enquiry he learnt of his or her death. He said: 'Why did you not tell me about her? Show me her grave.' He went to the woman's grave and prayed for her." (Related by al-Bukhari and Muslim)

Al-Bukhari follows this hadith by quoting Ibn 'Abbās who commented: "I vow to You what is in my womb to serve the mosque. This refers to the Qur'anic verse which says: 'My Lord, I vow to You that which is in my womb, to be devoted to Your service.'" (3: 35) In *Fatḥ al-Bārī*, Ibn Ḥajar said: "Ibn Khuzaymah narrated this hadith on Abu Hurayrah's authority, stating without hesitation that she was 'a black woman.' Al-Bayhaqī related the hadith, stating that the woman was called Umm Miḥjan. The hadith also indicates that it was permissible in earlier divine religions to vow a child for such purpose. It appears that al-Bukhari related this hadith in his *Ṣaḥīḥ* to make clear that it was the practice of past communities to venerate a place of worship, serving it. The hadith is relevant to this chapter as it makes clear that a woman may dedicate herself to serving a mosque as the Prophet approved this.

**The twelfth and final purpose for which women went to the mosque was to sleep there.** 'Ā'ishah narrated that a certain family had a young black slave woman whom they set free. She went to the Prophet and declared her acceptance of Islam. A short tent made of hair was erected for her in the mosque, and she used to come to me for a chat. (Related by al-Bukhari) We should note that al-Bukhari enters this hadith under the heading: 'Women sleeping in the mosque.' This is followed by another chapter with the heading, 'Men sleeping in the mosque.' Under this latter heading he includes several hadiths one of which mentions that 'Abdullāh ibn 'Umar used to sleep in the Prophet's mosque when he was a young, unmarried man. Also, Abu Hurayrah reports that he saw no less than 70 of the people of *Ṣuffah* do so. These were poor people who stayed at *Ṣuffah*, at the mosque and the Prophet looked after them, ensuring that they were fed.

Commenting on the hadith narrated by 'Ā'ishah, Ibn Ḥajar says that it clearly indicates the permissibility of sleeping in the mosque if a Muslim man or woman is homeless, provided that no impropriety is feared.

All the hadiths that we have cited confirm that women used to go to the Prophet's mosque on all occasions and for all purposes. It is important, therefore, to point out the rules women should observe when attending the mosque, providing the evidence supporting them.

1. Women should wear no perfume when they go to the mosque. Zaynab, ʿAbdullāh ibn Masʿūd's wife reports: "The Prophet said to us: 'When any woman among you comes to the mosque, she should not wear perfume.'" (Related by Muslim) Ibn Daqīq al-ʿĪd comments that whatever is akin to perfume should be included in this restriction. The restriction is due to the fact that perfume may stir men's desire, and it may also stir a woman's desire. Therefore, what could cause the same effect should be included here. The Prophet is authentically reported to have said: "Any woman who has used incense should not attend our night prayer, i.e. ʿIshā'." The same applies to women's clothes and jewellery that are especially attractive.
2. Women's lines should be behind men's lines, with no partition in between. Fāṭimah bint Qays reports: "...I heard a crier carrying out the Prophet's instructions and calling for prayer followed by a public meeting. I went with the people to attend. I was in the first line of women, which is the one next to the last line of men." (Related by Muslim) Jābir ibn ʿAbdullāh narrated: "The sun was eclipsed during the Prophet's lifetime... He led the congregation in prayer, offering two *rakʿahs* with six bowings [i.e. bowing three times in each] and four prostrations [i.e. two in each]... He then stepped back and the lines fell behind him until we reached the women's lines..." (Related by Muslim)

Women should pray with the congregation, with their lines behind the men's lines, but without a partition. This is the guidance given to us by the Prophet. This was because there was no excessive sensitivity about men and women being in the same place. It was enough to distinguish them by the arrangement of their lines. Moreover, it was important that women should be able to follow the imam properly as he moved from one position to another. It was not enough that they heard him glorifying God to signal each move. He might do so and unwittingly rise for the third *rak'ah*, although he was supposed to sit down for *tashahhud*. Those who do not see him might have thought that he was sitting. Again, if the imam was reading a verse which required a prostration, and he signalled it, a listener who did not see him might think that he was signalling bowing, rather than a prostration. To make sure of the congregation following him, the Prophet said to them when he noticed that their lines were a little too far back: "Come forward and follow me, so that those who are behind you can follow you". This means that each line should be able to see the line before them. Thus, the first of women's lines follow the last of the men's lines.

Al-Sarakhsī, a leading Hanafi scholar, says: "A high wall, with no gap, separating the imam from those behind the wall does not permit a proper congregation."

We read in *al-Mudawwanah* what Ibn al-Qāsim reports: "I asked Mālik about a group of people coming to the mosque only to find that the open area is filled by women's lines, while the front area is filled with men's lines. This group formed a line behind the women's lines and joined the congregation. Is their prayer valid?" Mālik said: "Yes, their prayer is valid and complete. They do not need to repeat it."

3. The best of women's lines is the last one. Abu Hurayrah narrated: "The best of men's lines is the first and the worst is the last, while the best of women's lines is the last and the worst is the first." (Related by Muslim) This is not to suggest that all contact between men and women in the mosque is improper. It simply highlights practical considerations.

Those in the first line are the ones who come early to the mosque. They stand close to the imam and as such they can follow the recitation of the Qur'an more attentively. By contrast, a woman may find it hard to come early, because she has to attend to things at home particularly if she has young children. Moreover, being close to men's lines may be distracting to either party. This organisation has a further advantage, which is preventing crowding at the mosque's entrance. It also enables women to be the first to leave after the prayer is over. Thus, women can be the last to arrive in the mosque and the first to leave. This reflects care for women and consideration for their domestic responsibilities.

4. Women are recommended to wait a little before raising their heads after prostration. Sahl ibn Sa'd reports: "Men used to pray with the Prophet tying their robes around their necks. Therefore, women were told not to lift their heads [from prostration] until men had sat down." (Related by al-Bukhari and Muslim) The reason for this, according to Ibn Ḥajar, was to avoid the possibility that women would see men's private parts as these might be exposed when they rise. When men's robes are tied around their necks, they cover less of their bodies, leaving that possibility. The same principle applies today when some men wear tight trousers.

5. Drawing attention by clapping. Sahl ibn Sa'd quotes the Prophet as saying: "What is the matter with you clapping so often? If there is something to which you want to draw the imam's attention you should glorify God, saying *Subḥān Allah*. Clapping is for women only." (Related by al-Bukhari and Muslim) This is when a woman wants to draw the imam's attention to a mistake he might have made, or to something nearby which he cannot see.

6. The imam should make sure to facilitate things for women, particularly in 'Ishā' Prayer which should not be delayed. 'Ā'ishah narrated: "One night the Prophet was late for 'Ishā'

Prayer, until 'Umar called out to him saying: 'Women and children are overcome by sleep.' The Prophet went to the mosque to lead the prayer. He said: 'No one on the face of the earth is waiting for this prayer other than you.' At the time, Madinah was the only place where people prayed. They used to offer this prayer between the disappearance of the bright horizon and the end of the first third of the night." (Related by al-Bukhari and Muslim)

7. Keeping the congregational prayer short. Anas ibn Mālik quotes the Prophet as saying: "I may begin a prayer intending to make it long. Then I may hear a child crying, and I keep the prayer short because I realize that his mother is anxious to attend to him." (Related by al-Bukhari and Muslim)
8. Giving women a chance to leave first. Hind bint al-Ḥārith quotes Umm Salamah, the Prophet's wife, as saying: "When the congregational prayer finished during the Prophet's lifetime, women would quickly rise and leave, while the Prophet and the men who were with him in the prayer would wait for a while. When the Prophet rose, the men also rose." Another version says: "When the Prophet finished a prayer with *salām*, the women left immediately after, but he stayed for a short while before he rose." (Related by al-Bukhari) Al-Zuhrī comments: "I believe that the Prophet stayed behind a little to allow women to leave before men."
9. There is no restriction preventing men and women from dealing with one another in the mosque. For one thing, they see each other, since there is no screen or separation between their places of worship. People used to lower their gaze, but they could look casually at each other. There is nothing wrong with this. Moreover, the hadiths that we have quoted make clear that conversation between men and women took place when needed. We quoted the hadith speaking of women being told to stay a little longer before raising their heads in prayer. One hadith mentions that in one quarter, the imam

was a child wearing a short robe. He was chosen because he had learnt more of the Qur'an than anyone else in his clan. One woman pointed out that he needed longer robes, and the men bought a new one for him. Another hadith quotes a woman companion of the Prophet: 'I said to a man who was close to me: "May God bless you; what was the last thing the Prophet said?"

> There are also hadiths which indicate that men and women moved freely in the mosque. We mentioned the hadith of the woman who used to clean the mosque and when the Prophet missed her he was told that she had died. He said to his companions that they should have mentioned her death to him. He wanted to know where she was buried and he went to her grave, praying there for her.

Men and women moved freely and talked to each other in the mosque. Al-Bukhari includes in his *Ṣaḥīḥ* a chapter on sharing and hanging donations in the mosque. Ibn Ḥajar comments:

> "Al-Bukhari does not include in this chapter any hadith about hanging a bunch of dates in the mosque. He considers it to come under the same heading as placing charity money in the mosque, because in both cases it is offered for the poor. He, thus, refers to a hadith related by al-Nasā'ī: 'God's Messenger came out holding a stick in his hand. A man had hung up a bunch of tasteless dry dates. The Prophet hit that bunch and said: "Had the man wished, he could have donated something better than this."' This hadith does not meet al-Bukhari's conditions, although it has a sound chain of transmission. Under the same heading we have a different hadith which says: 'The Prophet ordered that a bunch of dates should be hung on every wall in the mosque,' which means that it is offered

for the poor. Another version mentions that Mu'ādh ibn Jabal was in charge of these to make them available or to divide them."

If these bunches of dates were hung in the mosque so that poor people would take from them, such poor people included men and women.

We may remind ourselves of the hadith concerning the woman – or the man – who used to clean the mosque, and the hadith that a maid had a small tent in the mosque where she used to sleep at night. We also remember the hadith narrated by al-Rubayyi' concerning the fasting of 10 Muharram, and taking the fasting young children to the mosque, giving them soft dolls when they complained of hunger. A well-known story mentions that 'Umar urged people not to ask excessive dowries for their daughters, and a woman objected to him. This serves as an example of implementation, even though its chain of transmission is not particularly strong.

After this long discussion of women frequenting the Prophet's mosque during his lifetime, it is very useful to consider his reaction to women's presence in his mosque, remembering that whatever the Prophet taught was and remains good and beneficial. We find him on one occasion delaying the obligatory prayer of 'Ishā'. Such a delay is good because it makes it part of night worship, and a good conclusion to a day's activities. However, when someone said that women and children were falling asleep, he immediately went out to lead the congregational prayer, so that he would not cause women and children more hardship in waiting for that prayer. On another occasion, he started his prayer intending to make it long. Again this is good because the closest position to God we can attain is when we are in prayer. However, he heard a child crying and he made his prayer short, realizing that the child's mother wanted to attend to her child. If she were to remain long in prayer she might find this exceedingly difficult. Thus, we see that the Prophet was always kind to all people and very compassionate.

At one point a woman was raped when she was on her way to the mosque for Fajr Prayer, but this did not result in any restriction imposed on women's attending Fajr Prayers in the mosque, nor indeed any prayer at night or day. On the contrary, women will benefit by listening to the Qur'an being recited in Fajr Prayer, particularly when the imam reads long passages of the Qur'an in his prayer. Nor did the Prophet ever issue an order to women preventing them from taking their young children to the mosque with them. It might happen that a woman could not find anyone to take care of her child during her absence from home attending prayer at the mosque. Her only option if she wanted to attend the prayer was to take her child with her. There was no harm in this.

All this makes clear that despite the position of distinction given to women, the doors of all mosques should be kept open for women in the same way as they are open for men. No one may claim to be more protective of the honour of the Muslim community and its members than the Prophet. No one may say that he is more eager than him to see God's law implemented. What should be remembered is that the Prophet was also eager that women should have their chance to have the sort of knowledge that keeps their minds alive.

Can we claim that our women today do not need the sort of education that the Prophet's female companions sought when they frequented the mosque to listen to the Qur'an being recited in prayer and to the Prophet's admonition? Do they not need to have the religious education the Prophet's female companions acquired from him? Scholars are the heirs to the messages of prophets. Our women cannot gain their knowledge from the Prophet directly, but they can certainly acquire it through his heirs. To suggest that their parents or husbands can give them such knowledge is a non-starter. Needless to say, not every parent or husband can teach or give effective admonition. Yet people claim that the moral fabric of society has greatly weakened. In reply we say that one way for it to regain its strength is to encourage women to frequently go to mosques.

What is permissible and left as a matter of choice may become recommended or even a duty in certain situations. Modern societies have tended to steadily move away from religion in all aspects where women are concerned: in school, radio, television, magazines, social customs and traditions. Therefore, our women have a stronger need to attend the mosque as frequently as possible, at any time, for all prayers particularly Friday Prayer. They should go there to listen to lectures and religious discussion whenever they can. They should also attend the Tarāwīḥ Prayer during Ramadan, when long passages of the Qur'an are recited. This provides special enjoyment. Women today are subjected to an onslaught that can only be countered by intellectual and spiritual immunization. Their natural tendency to goodness must be enhanced so that they can be more active in doing what is good and beneficial. They need to have their own clean and sound environment, where good and religious women can meet and get to know each other. They will, thus, have a chance to strengthen their resolve to live in accordance with Islamic teachings, resisting all influences that try to tempt them away from them.

The hadith that says, "Do not deprive women from having their share in mosques," lays down an important rule. While a woman's attendance at the mosque may be permissible in certain situations, rising to the rank of what is encouraged or even a duty in others, it is not permissible for a woman's husband or father to prevent her from such attendance. Their guardianship of women does not extend to this. On the contrary, they should encourage them to do so. Let men remember the Prophet's instructions: "If I forbid you something, you must refrain from it."

It is extremely unfortunate that we see such prevention happening at both individual and societal levels. Women have been prevented by society from attending mosques over many centuries. This was a first step in discarding the Prophet's teachings, negating the role of Muslim women in all social activities: worship, education, jihad and entertainment. During the Prophet's lifetime, women admirably fulfilled that role. In later generations, they gradually lost it until they became confined within the walls of their parents' or husbands' homes. This move away from the Prophet's sunnah has led to a steady weakening of the Muslim woman's personality. As generations passed, the gulf between her personality and that of her counterpart during the Prophet's lifetime has greatly widened, giving her a distorted image of a weak mind, lax morality and narrow-mindedness.

## Participation in the Pursuit of Knowledge

There are many hadiths that show that the Prophet's wives and female companions eagerly sought knowledge, showing the same determination Muslim men showed. These hadiths span the entire period from the very early days of the Islamic message up to the end of the Prophet's blessed life. Muslim women continued to pursue knowledge afterwards, until their position in society started to decline as a result of different factors. We will quote here several of these hadiths and comment on one or two of them in order to provide a full picture. The first hadith is a long one, narrated by 'Ā'ishah, explaining the Prophet's reaction when he received his first revelation, meeting the Angel Gabriel for the first time, and the reassurance he needed. The report is very long, but we will quote only the part showing how Khadījah, the Prophet's first wife, sought to provide him with such reassurance:

"Then Khadījah took him to Waraqah ibn Nawfal, her paternal cousin who was a Christian convert and a scholar with good knowledge of

Arabic, Hebrew and the Bible. He had lost his eyesight, as he had grown very old. Khadījah said to Waraqah: 'Cousin, would you like to hear what your nephew has to say?' [Waraqah was not, in fact, the Prophet's uncle. Khadījah's reference to Muhammad as his nephew was in accordance with the standards of politeness prevailing in Arabia at the time.] Waraqah said: 'Well, nephew, what have you seen?' The Prophet related to him what he saw [at Ḥirā' cave at the start of revelations]. When he had finished, Waraqah said: 'It is the same revelation as was sent down to Moses. I wish I was a young man so that I might be alive when your people turn you away from this city.' The Prophet exclaimed: 'Would they turn me away?' Waraqah answered: 'Yes! No man has ever preached a message like yours and was not met with enmity. If I live till that day, I will certainly give you all my support.'" (Related by al-Bukhari and Muslim)

Ibn Jurayj was one of the early scholars of hadith, belonging to the second generation after that of the Prophet's companions. He reports a hadith he learnt from 'Aṭā' on the authority of Jābir ibn 'Abdullāh, a companion of the Prophet. As reported by Ibn Jurayj, the hadith includes clarifications he sought from 'Aṭā' and the latter's answers. The hadith mentions that on one Eid occasion when the Prophet finished his sermon, he realized that women might have not heard his speech after the prayer. "... Therefore, the Prophet went to the women present and spoke to them, reminding them of their Islamic duties, as he leaned on Bilāl's arm. Bilāl held up his robe so that women could put in it whatever they wanted to give as *sadaqah*, or charity." I said to 'Aṭā': "Was this Zakat al-Fiṭr?" He said: "No. It was just a charity they might wish to donate on that occasion. Women gave away their special rings." I said: "Do you think that it is a duty of the ruler to thus remind women?" He said: "It is certainly a duty required of Muslim rulers. Why are they not doing it nowadays?" (Related by al-Bukhari and Muslim)

Ibn Ḥajar refers to the fact that al-Bukhari enters this hadith under the heading, 'A ruler's admonition of women on Eid Day.' He adds: "Thus al-Bukhari is drawing attention to the fact that what was mentioned about providing one's family with education is not limited to the home and family. It is indeed recommended for the ruler or whoever deputises for him to do so." *Qadi* 'Iyāḍ claims that the Prophet's admonition of women was made during his speech, and that it occurred during the early days of Islam, and that such ability to admonish was a privilege given to the Prophet only. However, al-Nawawī refutes 'Iyāḍ's claims, citing this report which clearly states 'when he finished, the Prophet went to the women...' He further adds that special privileges cannot be claimed merely on the basis of probability. 'Aṭā' said: "It is certainly a duty," which suggests that 'Aṭā' considered it a binding duty of the ruler. Hence, taking the opposite view, 'Iyāḍ said: "No one else shares this view." Al-Nawawī, on the other hand, said this is acceptable if it does not lead to a negative result.

As for 'Iyāḍ's claim that this was delivered during the early days of Islam, we say that Ibn 'Abbās was present on this particular occasion. Ibn 'Abbās only migrated to Madinah after Makkah had fallen to Islam in the eighth year of the Prophet's arrival there, i.e. two years before he passed away. Thus, it could not have taken place in the early days, but rather towards the end of Islamic revelations.

Another example of women seeking to learn the rulings of Islam on whatever question may pertain to their situations is provided by Zaynab, 'Abdullāh ibn Mas'ūd's wife. He was poor while she had an income. She supported her husband as well as some orphans who were related to her. "I said to 'Abdullāh: 'Ask the Prophet if my support of you and the orphans I am bringing up pays off my zakat duty.' He said to me: 'You ask God's Messenger.' I went to the Prophet and found at his door a woman from the Anṣār coming to ask the same question. Bilāl passed by us, and we requested him to ask the Prophet on our behalf if my zakat is deemed to be paid by my support of my husband and orphans. We also said to him not to mention us by name. Bilāl went in and asked the Prophet our question. The Prophet asked him: 'Who are they?' He said: 'Zaynab.' The Prophet asked: 'Which Zaynab?' He said: ''Abdullāh's wife.' He said: 'Yes, it is enough. She earns double reward: one for being kind to relatives and one for paying her zakat.'" (Related by al-Bukhari and Muslim)

Needless to say, it was through such questions about actual life situations that we have learnt much of what Islam requires, approves or prohibits. When people went to the Prophet with their questions, he provided them with guidance that applies to all those who are in similar circumstances. Women went to the Prophet with all sorts of questions, even those that were most private. 'Ā'ishah narrated: "Fāṭimah bint Abi Ḥubaysh came to the Prophet and said: 'Messenger of God! I bleed continuously and my discharge does not cease. Should I stop praying?' The Prophet said: 'No. This bleeding is due to a particular vein; it is not menses. When your period starts,[3] stop praying until it is over when you should wash off the blood, take a bath and pray. Then you need to have a fresh ablution, i.e. *wudu*, for every prayer.'" (Related by al-Bukhari and Muslim)

The Prophet's companions realized that by adopting Islam, they committed themselves to a fundamental change in their life patterns and the way they conducted their affairs. Hence, they went to him asking about everything that occurred to them. Men and women sought his guidance. Therefore, it was not uncommon that they should meet and exchange information, or discuss matters. They found nothing wrong with this. Nor did the Prophet at any time point to any need for separation between men and women.

---

3. In a different hadith, the Prophet tells women that such bleeding can be distinguished from menses by its colour. Menses is darker and thicker, while *istiḥāḍah* discharge is lighter red and thinner.

Abu Mūsā al-Ash'arī narrated: "...When the Prophet came in, she [Asmā' bint 'Umays] said: 'God's Messenger! 'Umar has just said, "We have had the honour of migrating with the Prophet before you. We have a better claim to God's Messenger (peace be upon him) than you." The Prophet asked her, 'What was your reply to him?' She reported her answer saying: 'No, by God. You were with God's Messenger (peace be upon him) who fed those of you who were hungry and admonished the ignorant, while we were in the land of hostile strangers, staying there only for the sake of God and His Messenger... We were often subjected to harm and we were scared.' The Prophet said: 'He does not have a better claim to me than you. He and his fellow Muslims have the reward of one migration, while you, the people of the boat, shall have the reward of two migrations.' Asmā' added: 'Abu Mūsā and the people who came on the boat from Abyssinia came in groups to see me asking about this hadith. Nothing in this world gave them more joy and greater happiness than what God's Messenger said about them.'" Abu Burdah said that Asmā' said: "Abu Mūsā came over requesting that I narrate the hadith to him again." (Related by al-Bukhari and Muslim)

'Āmir al-Sha'bī said that he asked Fāṭimah bint Qays, who was one of the early Muslim women to migrate: "Tell me a hadith which you yourself heard from the Prophet, not reporting it through anyone else." She said she could easily do so if she had a mind to. He insisted and she reported to him the following hadith: "I heard the caller announcing prayer to be held shortly [which meant that a public meeting would be held]. I went out to the mosque and joined the Prophet's prayer. I was in the women's row that was immediately behind the men's rows. When the Prophet finished the prayer, he sat on the platform smiling. He said: 'Let everyone stay where they are. Do you know why I have asked you to come?' They said: 'God and His Messenger know best.' He said: 'I have not asked you to come in order to announce anything pleasant or unpleasant. I only want to tell you that Tamīm al-Dārī was a Christian man who came forward and declared himself a Muslim, pledging his allegiance to me. He told me something that was in agreement with what I had told you about the Impostor who would claim to be the Messiah. He said to me that he went on a boat in the sea with thirty people...'" (Related by Muslim)

The hadith goes on to report what the Prophet said, but we are now interested only in this first part which makes clear that men and women were equal in seeking knowledge and that they met as they pursued what they sought. Here, Fāṭimah mentions that she was in the first of the women's rows and listened to the Prophet as he gave them this information.

In fact, the Prophet's companions did not find it odd that they should seek knowledge from the opposite sex. Ṭāwūs, a famous scholar of the *tābi'īn* generation, reports: "I was with Ibn 'Abbās when Zayd ibn Thābit said to him: 'Did you rule that a woman pilgrim who is having her period could leave before she has performed the *ṭawāf* of farewell?' Ibn 'Abbās said: 'If you are unsure, then go and ask this Anṣārī woman [he named her] whether it was God's Messenger who ordered her to do so.' When Zayd ibn Thābit returned to meet again with Ibn 'Abbās he said to him: 'I see that you have said the truth.'" (Related by Muslim)

This is just one example of men seeking to learn from women. We mentioned many other examples when we discussed how the Prophet's companions sought to learn from his wives what he had said about different issues. Needless to say, when the Prophet travelled for his pilgrimage, there were many occasions when men and women met and exchanged information, or learnt together from the Prophet. Here are three examples, the first of which suggests that the Prophet gave a general order, applying to men and women alike:

'Ā'ishah narrated: "We went out with the Prophet on his Farewell Pilgrimage. We all declared our intention to perform the *'umrah.*

Then the Prophet announced: 'Whoever has brought his sacrifice with him should declare their intention to do the hajj and the '*umrah* together. They must not release themselves from consecration until they have done their duties for both.'" (Related by al-Bukhari and Muslim)

Yaḥyā ibn al-Ḥuṣayn quotes his grandmother, Umm al-Ḥuṣayn: "I went out with the Prophet on his Farewell Pilgrimage. I saw him when he did the stoning at Jamrat al-'Aqabah and then left. He was on his camel, and Bilāl and Usāmah were with him. One of them was leading the camel and the other holding his robe above the Prophet's head to shelter him from the sun. The Prophet said many things, before I heard him saying: 'If a slave whose ears and nose have been cut (and the reporter thought that she described the slave as 'black') is appointed your leader and he implements God's Book, then you must listen and obey him.'" (Related by Muslim)

Ibn 'Abbās narrated that the Prophet met a group of travellers at al-Rawḥā' and asked them who they were. They said: "We are Muslims. Who are you?" He said: "I am God's Messenger." A woman lifted her baby son and asked him: "Can this one perform the hajj?" He said: "Yes, and you earn a reward." (Related by Muslim)

## Participation in Jihad

Under the major heading of jihad, hadith anthologies enter many sub-headings, each dealing with a particular aspect. As al-Bukhari is particularly selective in his sub-headings, he often highlights certain aspects even though they may not be very clear in the hadith texts that are entered under that sub-heading. In this way, he draws attention to a particular point. Therefore, we will quote one hadith from each of five sub-headings, indicating women's participation in the ultimate aspect of striving for God's cause, i.e. jihad, which is fighting the enemies of Islam.

1. **Praying for men's and women's participation in jihad and martyrdom**. Anas ibn Mālik reports: "The Prophet used to visit Umm Ḥarām bint Milḥān... He once slept [at her place] and when he woke up, he smiled. She asked him what caused him to smile. He said: 'I was shown a group of my followers going out for jihad, riding into the sea, looking like kings on their thrones...' She said: 'Messenger of God! Pray to God to make me one of them.' He prayed for her as she requested. He then put his head down and slept. He woke up smiling. She said: 'What makes you smile, Messenger of God?' He again said the same thing: 'I was shown a group of my followers going out for jihad...' She said: 'Messenger of God! Pray to God to make me one of them.' He said: 'You are one of the first group.' She went on the maritime expedition during the reign of Muʿāwiyah ibn Abi Sufyān, and when she disembarked, she fell off her mount and died." (Related by al-Bukhari and Muslim)

2. **Women's participation in fighting with men**. Anas reports: "During the Battle of Uhud, Muslims went on the retreat, leaving the Prophet... I saw ʿĀ'ishah and Umm Sulaym, having raised their skirts. I could see their anklets as they carried waterskins on their backs, hurrying as though to run... They would pour the water into people's mouths and go back to fill their waterskins. They came back to pour the water into people's mouths." (Related by al-Bukhari and Muslim)

Commenting on this point, Ibn Ḥajar says that he did not find in any of the hadiths entered under this sub-heading a clear statement that women actually participated in fighting. Therefore, Ibn al-Munīr says: "Al-Bukhari has put it in his heading, but the hadiths do not indicate this. He either means that the assistance they provided to the fighters is, in itself, a form of fighting or he means that when they actually remained steadfast to give water to the wounded and render other services, they meant to defend themselves in case there was need. This second possibility is perhaps stronger." Indeed, Muslim relates a hadith in which it is mentioned that Umm Sulaym had a dagger at the time of the Battle of Ḥunayn. She explained: "I need it, so that if any of the unbelievers comes near me, I will use my dagger to stab him in his abdomen."

3. **Women carrying water for the fighters.** Thaʿlabah ibn Mālik reports: "ʿUmar distributed some cloth among some women of Madinah. One good piece of cloth was left. Someone present suggested that he give it 'to the Prophet's granddaughter you have married', [meaning Umm Kulthūm bint ʿAlī]. ʿUmar said: 'Umm Salīṭ [a woman from the Anṣār] has a stronger claim to it. She carried water to us during the Battle of Uhud." (Related by al-Bukhari)
4. **Treating the wounded in war.** Al-Rubayyiʿ bint Muʿawwidh narrated: "We used to go on jihad with the Prophet, providing water for the fighters to drink and treatment for the wounded..." (Related by al-Bukhari)
5. **Sending back the wounded and the dead.** Al-Rubayyiʿ bint Muʿawwidh narrated: "We used to go on jihad with the Prophet, providing water for the fighters to drink and serving them. We also sent the wounded and the dead ones back to Madinah." (Related by al-Bukhari)

According to the reports given in Ibn Saʿd's *al-Ṭabaqat*, the number of women who participated in the Battle of Khaybar was 15. Their names are given in full. They are: Umm Sinān of the Aslam clan, Umm Ayman, Salmā who was married to Abu Rāfiʿ, Kuʿaybah bint Saʿd of Aslam, Umm Muṭaʿ of Aslam, Umayyah bint Qays of Ghifār, Umm Āmir of ʿAbd al-Ashhal, Umm al-Ḍaḥḥāk bint Masʿūd of al-Ḥārith, Hind bint ʿAmr ibn Ḥarām, Umm manīʿ bint ʿAmr, Umm ʿUmārah Nasībah bint Kaʿb, Umm Salīṭ of al-Najjār, Umm Sulaym, Umm ʿAṭiyyah of the Anṣār and Umm al-ʿAlāʾ of the Anṣār.

We learn for example that Umm Sulaym was one of them. Confirmation of her participation in this battle is given in a hadith reported by Anas in which he says: "The Prophet freed Ṣafiyyah and married her... When the Prophet had marched some distance on his way back, Umm Sulaym assisted her in preparations for her wedding to the Prophet..." (Related by al-Bukhari and Muslim)

All these hadiths confirm that women joined the Prophet on his jihad campaigns, rendering important services during battle. It is certain that Islam does not require women to fight for God's cause in the same way as men are required. Fighting is very hard and requires physical strength that may be beyond most women. It also needs an attitude that does not fit with women's softer nature. Yet, Islam allows women to volunteer to fight or join a military force going on jihad, even though the number of male fighters is sufficient. This applies when participation in fighting is a collective duty on the whole community. In this case, when sufficient numbers of men are taking part, the others are exempt. Should fighting become an individual duty and the numbers of male fighters are not sufficient, women who can are required to take part as a duty.

We see that Islam does not stop women from entertaining ambitions to achieve great distinction in every way. It opens all doors for them. Ibn Ḥajar quotes Ibn Baṭṭāl, a distinguished scholar, as saying: "Jihad is not a duty required of women. However, when the Prophet said to women, 'Your jihad is to go on pilgrimage,' he did not stop them from volunteering to join jihad campaigns, but to do so is not their binding duty."

## Meeting When Giving Advice

During the Prophet's lifetime men and women met frequently, in all situations. This was accepted as normal. The Prophet did not issue any instructions to prevent such get togethers. In fact, he dealt with it as perfectly normal. He only encouraged people to perform their duty of enjoining what is right and forbidding what is wrong. Again this applies to all Muslims, across all situations. God describes believers in the following terms: "The believers, men and women, are friends to one another: They enjoin what is right and forbid what is wrong; they attend to their prayers, and pay their zakat, and obey God and His Messenger. It is on these that God will have mercy. Surely, God is Almighty, Wise." (9: 71) This verse clearly indicates that there is no difference between men and women in these qualities. Enjoining what is right and forbidding what is wrong is thus a quality that all Muslims should have at all times. When we consider how life was in the first Muslim society established by the Prophet we find this quality operating all the time. Here are a few relevant hadiths:

Jābir narrated: "The Prophet visited Umm Mubashshir, one of his Anṣārī companions, on her date farm. He asked her: 'Who planted these date trees: was he a Muslim or an unbeliever?' She said: 'A Muslim.' He said: 'Whenever a Muslim plants something and a man or animal eats of its fruit, he will have that credited to him as a *ṣadaqah*, or charity.'" (Related by Muslim) The relevance of this hadith to the question we are discussing is that the Prophet's statement encourages kindness to all.

Anas ibn Mālik reports: "The Prophet passed by a woman who was crying hard near a grave. He said to her: 'Fear God and be patient in your adversity.' She said: 'Leave me alone. You have not experienced the like of my tragedy.' She apparently did not recognize the Prophet. She was told, [after he had left], that he was the Prophet. Therefore, she went to see him, but she found that he had no doorkeeper. When she met him, she said to him: 'I did not recognize you.' He said to her: 'True patience is that shown when the first shock is received.'" (Related by al-Bukhari and Muslim)

It should be noted that al-Bukhari enters a shorter version of this hadith under the heading, 'A man says to a woman by the side of a grave to be patient.' Ibn Ḥajar quotes al-Zayn ibn al-Munīr's comment that al-Bukhari's usage of 'a man' in his heading is intended to indicate that this applies to all people, and it is not a special privilege granted to the Prophet. Indeed it is perfectly permissible for men and women to exchange any words like these, enjoining what is right and forbidding what is wrong, or offering condolences, or good words of admonition. This is universally applicable to young and old alike, because it serves a good religious purpose.

Subay'ah bint al-Ḥārith reports that she was married to Sa'd ibn Khawlah who was one of the Prophet's companions who took part in the Battle of Badr. He died during the Prophet's Farewell Pilgrimage when she was pregnant. Only a few days after her husband's death, she gave birth. When she was out of confinement after delivery, she put on her make-up, hoping for a marriage proposal. Abu al-Sanābil ibn Ba'kak, a man from the 'Abd al-Dār clan, came to her and said: "How come you are wearing make-up; hoping to get married? By God, you cannot get married before the lapse of four months and ten days [after your husband's death]." (Related by al-Bukhari and Muslim)

The relevance here is that Abu al-Sanābil was admonishing a woman who was not related to him. We learn from other reports that he subsequently proposed marriage to her, but she declined. The point in dispute between them is the length of her waiting period. He thought she had to observe the full waiting period of four months and ten days. She, however, was aware that a pregnant woman finishes her waiting period upon giving birth, whether this takes place after a few days or nine months. Indeed, she went that evening to ask the Prophet about this point and he confirmed that she was free to marry again.

Another hadith gives us the opposite situation, with a woman admonishing a man who happened to be the caliph. 'Abd al-Malik ibn Marwān sent some cushions and other articles of furniture to Umm al-Dardā'. One night, he rose up at night and called his servant. It appears that the servant was slow in answering him. He cursed him. In the morning Umm al-Dardā' said to him: "I heard you last night cursing your servant when you called him. The Prophet said: 'Those who curse will not be allowed to intercede or act as witnesses on the Day of Judgement.'" (Related by Muslim)

All these hadiths confirm that men and women exchanged advice, encouraging what is right and forbidding what is wrong. Other hadiths show that such mixing also took place when providing a service or giving help. Jābir reports: "A woman from the Anṣār said to the Prophet: 'Shall I make something for you to sit on? I have a servant who is a carpenter.' The Prophet said to her: 'If you wish.' She got a platform made for him. The following Friday, the Prophet sat on the platform made for him." (Related by al-Bukhari)

Anas reports: "Any maid in Madinah could come to the Prophet and take him by the hand, taking him wherever she wished." (Related by al-Bukhari) Another version of this hadith is given by Ahmad, stating that such a maid would take the Prophet 'to give whatever help she wanted.' Al-Nasā'ī relates on the authority of 'Abdullāh ibn Abi Awfā: "God's Messenger did not disdain going with any widow or poor person and doing for them whatever they needed."

A hadith that is more relevant to the point we are discussing is reported by Asmā' bint Abu Bakr. It shows her pointing the way for a poor man to get round her husband's opposition to him establishing a position for business next to her home. She said: "...A man said to me: 'I am a poor person. Can I take a position here in the shade of your home where I can sell things?' I said: 'If I were to give you permission now, al-Zubayr [her husband] would not allow it. Your best way is to come and ask me when he is present.' He came over and addressed me saying: 'I am a poor person. May I sit and sell things in the shade of your home?' I retorted: 'Is there no place in Madinah where you can sell other than my home?' Al-Zubayr said to me: 'Will you stop a poor man trying to earn a living?' He continued to sell and made some money. I sold him my slave. Al-Zubayr came in when I had its price with me. He said: 'Give her to me as a gift.' I said: 'I have given her away as charity, i.e. *ṣadaqah*.'" (Related by Muslim)

## When Looking for a Spouse

In most societies, the normal practice is for the prospective husband to propose marriage. A woman normally holds back from suggesting marriage, feeling that she should be sought after. This applies to families as well. The Prophet received proposals from several women who thought that they could not do better than being married to him. This normally took the form of the woman saying to the Prophet that she would gift herself to him. The gift being understood as marriage. Although in Islam, a woman cannot gift herself to a man in this way, this was allowed for the Prophet. Only the Prophet could take her as a wife, but he normally made the decision to act as her guardian. This special privilege given to the Prophet is stated in the Qur'an: "And any believing woman who offers herself freely to the Prophet and whom the Prophet might be willing to wed: [this latter] applies to you alone and not to other believers." (33: 50)

Needless to say, at the time when a proposal of marriage is made, the man and the woman will need to meet and discuss matters in order to carry the proposal forward or withdraw it. Sahl ibn Sa'd reports: "A woman came to the Prophet and said: 'Messenger of God! I have come to offer myself to you as a gift...' The Prophet repeatedly looked up and down at her, then he lowered his head. When the woman realized that he had made no decision concerning her, she sat down." (Related by al-Bukhari and Muslim) Another version of this hadith adds that the Prophet said to her: "I have no need for women nowadays."

Commenting on this hadith, Imam Ibn Ḥajar says: "This hadith gives us several important points... One of these is the permissibility of looking carefully at a woman's attractions when one is thinking of marrying her, even though such thoughts of marriage were not entertained earlier, nor had a proposal been made. We see that the Prophet looked repeatedly at the woman, moving his gaze up and down. The hadith is stated in a way that implies a serious, long look. Needless to say, the Prophet did not consider marrying this woman prior to her proposal. He, indeed, told her that he had no desire at the time to enter into a new marriage. Yet he looked seriously at her, which suggests that had he seen in her something that was attractive to him, he would have married her. Otherwise, he would not have looked so intently at her."

Ibn Hajar suggests that the hadith may be understood in other ways. We, however, prefer the view we have quoted, because this is supported by other hadiths that encourage looking at a woman if one intends to marry her. The present case is not dissimilar to that of a man making a proposal. This is supported by the following hadith: "When the Muslims from Makkah arrived in Madinah, the Prophet established a bond of brotherhood between them and the Muslims from Madinah. He made 'Abd al-Raḥmān ibn 'Awf and Sa'd ibn al-Rabī' brothers. Sa'd said to 'Abd al-Raḥmān: 'I am one of the richest people among the Anṣār. I will share my wealth equally with you. I also have two wives. Look at them and tell me which one you prefer. I will divorce her and when she finishes her waiting period, you can marry her.' 'Abd al-Raḥmān said: 'May God give you much blessing in both your family and your wealth...'" (Related by al-Bukhari) Ibn Ḥajar comments that this hadith confirms that it is proper that a man looks carefully at a woman when he wants to propose marriage to her.

Perhaps we should add here that 'Abd al-Raḥmān ibn 'Awf was as noble as his brother. He declined to take any money, but started a business of his own to earn his living. Nor did he take up the offer of marrying one of his brother's wives after her suggested divorce. Instead, when his business took off, he married someone else.

It is also permissible for a woman to propose marriage to a man whom she thinks to be a good husband. Thābit al-Bunānī reports: "I was at Anas's place, with one of his daughters present. Anas mentioned that a woman came to the Prophet offering to marry him. She said: 'Messenger of God! Would you like to marry me?' Anas's daughter said: 'How shameless of her!' He said to her: 'She is better than you. She wished to marry the Prophet and she went to him suggesting that.'" (Related by al-Bukhari)

Al-Bukhari enters this hadith under the heading: 'A woman's proposal to marry a good man.' In his commentary on this hadith, Ibn Ḥajar quotes Ibn al-Munīr: "A subtle note by al-Bukhari is that, realizing the special privilege involved in this hadith, he highlighted what is generally applicable, representing no privilege, which is the permissibility of a woman making a proposal to a good and pious man, thinking that she will be happy with him because of his piety." Ibn Ḥajar adds: "There is nothing to be taken against a woman who wishes to marry someone who is in a better position than herself, particularly if her motive is a good one, either because the man is virtuous, or because she admires him to the point that it is feared that something wrong may happen unless such a proposal is made." Ibn Daqīq al-'Īd said: "The hadith indicates the permissibility of a woman offering marriage to a man with whom she hopes to have a blessed life."

We may add here a verse from the Qur'an mentioning a proposal made to a man by the father of a pious woman. The man concerned is Moses, but this took place long before he became a prophet. He had fled from Egypt where he was in danger of being killed. In Madyan, he helped two girls giving water to their sheep. Then one of them invited him to meet her father, who was a pious man. When the father learnt Moses' story, he offered one of his daughters to him in marriage. "[The father] said: 'I will give you one of these two daughters of mine in marriage on the understanding that you will remain eight years in my service. If you should complete ten years, it will be of your own choice. I do not wish to impose any hardship on you. You will find me, if God so wills, an upright man.'" (28: 27)

Moses accepted the proposal, married one of the girls and spent ten years helping her father. Needless to say, had there been anything unacceptable in this story, the Qur'an would have made that clear.

## Hinting at Marriage

In some Muslim communities, a woman is made to stay indoors throughout her waiting period, after her husband's death. A woman is certainly required to observe this waiting period, when she cannot marry someone else. For a widow, the waiting period lasts for four months and ten days, unless she is pregnant in which case the waiting period ends when she gives birth. The strict restrictions on a widow in her waiting period are largely social, which means that they are imposed by social tradition, rather than Islam. In some cases, women are not allowed to see even their close relatives until this period is over. Yet Islam permits a man to hint to this woman that he wishes to marry her. While he cannot make a direct proposal as long as she is in her waiting period, he can make a clear, unmistakable hint. This is stated in the Qur'an: "You will incur no sin if you give a hint of a marriage offer to [widowed] women or keep such an intention to yourselves. God knows that you will entertain such intentions concerning them. Do not, however, plight your troth in secret; but speak only in a decent manner. Furthermore, do not resolve on actually making the marriage tie before the prescribed term [of waiting] has run its course. Know well that God knows what is in your minds, so have fear of Him; and know that God is Much-Forgiving, Forbearing." (2: 235)

According to the well-known commentary on the Qur'an, *Tafsir al-Jalālayn*, authored by Jalāl al-Dīn al-Maḥallī and Jalāl al-Dīn al-Suyūṭī, a hint of a marriage offer may be that a man says to her: "You are pretty: who could find a woman like you?" Or, "There may be someone who wishes to marry you."

The Prophet himself dropped such a hint to a woman in her waiting period, even though he wanted her to marry someone he had in mind. Fāṭimah bint Qays, a woman from the early Muhājirīn, reports: "My husband Abu 'Amr ibn Ḥafṣ ibn al-Mughīrah sent me 'Ayyash ibn Abi Rabī'ah to inform me that he had divorced me. He sent with him five *ṣā's* of dates and five of barley. [The *ṣā'* was a measure equal to a little more than two kilograms.] I said to him: 'Is this all my maintenance? Am I not to observe my waiting period in your home?' He said: 'No.' I put on my clothes and went to see the Prophet. He asked me how many times I was divorced. I said: 'Three.' He said: 'He is right. You cannot claim maintenance. You can observe your waiting period at your cousin's home, Ibn Umm Maktūm. Since he is a blind man, you can take off your top garments in his home. When you finish your waiting period, let me know.'" (Related by Muslim) Another version of this hadith mentions that the Prophet sent her a word telling her not to get married without first informing him.

Al-Nawawi said: "The hadith indicates the permissibility of hinting at a forthcoming proposal to an irrevocably divorced woman. This is the correct view in our Shāfi'ī School." It is not surprising that the Prophet dropped such clear hints to this woman, because she was known to be a wise and pretty woman, in addition to her being among the early Muslims. The Prophet wanted her to marry Usāmah ibn Zayd, whom he loved dearly.

How do scholars understand the permission to drop a hint of marriage to a woman in her waiting period? Ibn 'Abbās comments on the verse that says, "You will incur no sin if you give a hint of a marriage offer to [widowed] women..." saying that a man may say to her, "I am keen to get married, and I hope that I will find a suitable woman." (Related by al-Bukhari)

Al-Ṭabarī, on the other hand, quotes several early scholars on this point. The first is another explanation by Ibn 'Abbās: "He may say to her, 'I would love to have a woman who is so and so, mentioning some good points.'" Mujāhid suggests: "He says to her, 'You are pretty; you will certainly have someone; you will indeed be in a good situation, etc.'" Al-Qāsim ibn Muhammad goes further: "He says: 'I am keen on you; I do care for you; I admire you, etc.'" Al-Suddī suggests: "He goes in, greets her and gives a present if he wishes, but says nothing."

Whichever view we take, there is strong evidence that a meeting between a woman in her waiting period and a man who wants to drop a hint of marriage is permissible. A different situation that allows such mixing is the actual intention to make a marriage proposal. God says in the Qur'an: "Those of you who die leaving wives behind, their wives shall wait, by themselves, for four months and ten days. When they have reached the end of their waiting-term, you shall incur no sin in whatever they may do with themselves in a lawful manner. God is aware of all that you do." (2: 234)

We note in the verse the part that reads, "You shall incur no sin in whatever they may do with themselves in a lawful manner." In *Tafsir al-Jalālayn*, this is explained as, "whatever they do of wearing make-up and hoping for a marriage proposal."

Subay'ah bint al-Ḥārith, a companion of the Prophet, reports that she was married to Sa'd ibn Khawlah, but he died during the Prophet's pilgrimage. Only a short while after that she gave birth to her child. When she regained her strength, she started to wear make-up expecting a proposal. Abu al-Sanābil ibn Ba'kak came to her and said: "How come you are adorned expecting a proposal, hoping to get married?..." (Related by al-Bukhari and Muslim) In another version, it was Abu al-Sanābil who proposed marrying her but she refused his proposal. Yet another version, related by Mālik in *Al-Muwaṭṭa'*, mentions that two people proposed to her, a young man and a middle aged one, but she preferred the younger man. The older one said to her that she was not free to marry. Apparently her people were away, and he hoped that if she delayed her marriage, they might prefer him when they returned.

Abu Hurayrah mentions that he was with the Prophet when a man came to tell him that he had just married a woman from the Anṣār. The Prophet asked him whether he looked at her before marriage. The man answered in the negative. The Prophet told him to go and look at her, because some of the Anṣār have something in their eyes.[4]

All these incidents confirm that Islam prefers that mixing at the time of making a marriage proposal is recommended. The following hadith relates to helping a poor young man to get married. Although the main thrust of the text is about giving such help, the incident itself is clear evidence that such mixing took place during the Prophet's lifetime and with his approval.

Sahl ibn Sa'd reports that a woman came to the Prophet and said to him: "Messenger of God, I have come to make of myself a gift to you." When the Prophet did not say anything to indicate his acceptance, a man said to him: "Messenger of God! If you do not propose to take her to yourself, marry her to me." The Prophet asked him whether he had anything to give her. The man said that he had nothing. The Prophet told him to go home and look for something to give her as a dowry. When the man came back, he reiterated that he had nothing.

---

4. This is a reference to some slight defect which may not be noticeable at a casual look. The Prophet wanted the man to make sure before the marriage was consummated.

The Prophet told him to try to find anything, even an iron ring. The man came back a second time to say that he could not find even an iron ring. He offered to give her half his robe. The Prophet said to him: "What use is that to her? If you wear it, she has nothing of it, and if she wears it, you will have nothing of it." The man sat down and then rose after a long while. When he turned away, the Prophet sent someone to call him back. He asked him whether he had learnt some parts of the Qur'an. The man said that he learnt several surahs. The Prophet asked him whether he knew them by heart. The man said: "Yes." The Prophet said to him: "I give her to you in marriage in return for [teaching her] what you have memorised of the Qur'an."

## Mixing on Social Occasions

Since people often speak about Islamic society being segregated, we need to assess how much segregation was practised in the Muslim society of Madinah. We will certainly find much that shows that society to have been a mixed one. A good indicator is found in the events of common joy, such as weddings and celebrations. The first such occasion was when the Prophet arrived in Madinah. Its people were awaiting his arrival with much anticipation. Abu Bakr reports: "We reached Madinah at night, and people disputed as to who would be the Prophet's host. He said: 'I will stay with the al-Najjar clan, the maternal uncles of 'Abd al-Muṭṭalib [the Prophet's grandfather]. They will take this as a favour.' Men and women were on top of their homes, and children and servants were in the roads calling out, 'O, Muhammad! O, Messenger of God! O, Muhammad! O, Messenger of God!'" (Related by Muslim)

Ibn 'Abbās reports on what he saw on the day Makkah fell to Islam and the Prophet entered the city: "People crowded around the Prophet saying: 'This is Muhammad! This is Muhammad!' Even young women came out of doors." (Related by Muslim)

Both of these occasions were public events in which we see men and women taking part alongside each other, with no objection from the Prophet. The two occasions took place eight years apart, which means that there was nothing in the Prophet's guidance throughout this period to prevent such participation. If it is said that the people of Makkah were not Muslim at the time, the Prophet would have pointed out to them that now that Islam was widely accepted in Makkah, their practice should not be repeated, but he did not.

'Ā'ishah narrated: "...When we arrived in Madinah, we settled among the clan of al-Ḥārith ibn Khazraj. I fell ill, and my hair fell out. Later it [increased and] became like a small bunch dropping to my shoulders. My mother, Umm Rūmān, came over and I was playing with my friends on a seesaw. She called me and I went to her, not knowing what she wanted. I was out of breath, so she stopped me at the door until I calmed down. She used some water to wipe my face and head, then she took me inside where there were several women from the Anṣār. They said: 'With all goodness and blessings! With all future happiness.' She left me with them and they attended to my appearance. All of a sudden I saw God's Messenger coming in when it was still mid-morning. They gave me up to him..." (Related by al-Bukhari and Muslim)

Al-Bukhari relates this hadith in a shorter version in the Book of Marriage, in a chapter with the heading: 'Supplication for the women preparing the bride and for the bride.' Ahmad relates a different version which includes: 'Ā'ishah said: "My mother brought me in... There was God's Messenger (peace be upon him) seated on his couch and surrounded by men and women from the Anṣār. She sat me very close to him and said: 'This is your bride, Messenger of God. May God make it a blessed marriage.' The men and women departed soon after and the Prophet consummated the marriage in our home."

Indeed we see the Prophet encouraging joyous celebration of weddings, particularly among the Anṣār whom he knew loved to have fun. ʿĀ'ishah reports: "I prepared a woman's wedding to a man from the Anṣār. The Prophet said to me: "ʿĀ'ishah, did you not have any entertainment? The Anṣār love to have entertainment.' (Related by al-Bukhari) In another version, the Prophet said to her: "You should have sent with the bride a maid to play the tambourine and sing."

We need to establish what the Prophet meant by entertainment. Perhaps we should look here at the usage of the same word in the Qur'anic verse speaking about people's behaviour at the time of prayer on Fridays. "Whenever they observe trade or entertainment, they scatter towards it, leaving you [Prophet] standing there. Say, 'What is with God is better than any entertainment or trade. God is the best provider.'" (62: 11) Al-Ṭabarī mentions several reports explaining this verse, but then he comments that the one reported by Jābir is perhaps the more accurate because he was one of them and saw these events. Jābir says: "When young women got married, a procession with drums and wood-wind instruments was organised. People would go to join these, leaving the Prophet giving his sermon. God then revealed the verse disapproving of their behaviour."

We find that playing music and singing was common practice at weddings in Madinah. Al-Rubayyiʿ bint Muʿawwidh reports: "The Prophet came to us when my wedding was over, and he sat on my bed, as close as you are seated now. Some maids of ours played the tambourine and sang, praising those of our people who were killed in the Battle of Badr. One of them said in her singing: 'Among us we have a Prophet who knows what will happen tomorrow.' The Prophet told her: 'Stop this and continue with what you were saying before.'" (Related by al-Bukhari)

In commenting on this hadith, Ibn Ḥajar quotes al-Muhallab: "This hadith confirms the desirability to publicise marriage by playing the tambourine and singing. It also indicates that the ruler may attend a wedding, even though it involves entertainment, as long as such entertainment remains within what is permissible."

Ibn Ḥajar also quotes a hadith related by al-Ṭabarānī quoting 'Ā'ishah: "The Prophet passed by women from the Anṣār celebrating a wedding and singing poetry that included a reference to someone as knowing what will happen tomorrow. He said: 'No one knows what will happen tomorrow other than God.'"

On both occasions we see the Prophet objecting to something said, because it is contrary to Islamic teachings and untrue. He did not object to the practice of singing or playing music on a joyous occasion such as a wedding. In fact, he encouraged this. When there was a wedding which his wife, 'Ā'ishah, organised, he told her that she should have arranged for some entertainment and singing. We also note that in Madinah men attended such singing at the time of weddings.

## Mixed Weddings

Let us look at the Qur'anic verse that requires the Prophet's wives to remain behind a screen when meeting men. Anas ibn Mālik says: "I am the one who knows best this verse and its revelation. When Zaynab bint Jaḥsh was wed to the Prophet and she was with him at home, he had food made and invited people to come. After having eaten, some people stayed on, engaged in conversation. [In the version related by Muslim, his wife was sitting with her face to the wall.] The Prophet went out and came back more than once, but they remained talking. Then God revealed the verse saying: 'Believers! Do not enter the Prophet's homes unless you are given leave for a meal without waiting for its proper time. But when you are invited, enter; and when you have eaten, disperse without lingering for the sake of mere talk. Such behaviour might give offence to the Prophet, and yet he might feel too shy to bid you go. God does not shy of stating what is right. When you ask the Prophet's wives for something, do so from behind a screen.' (33: 53) The people left, and this was how the Prophet's wives were screened." (Related by al-Bukhari and Muslim)

What is to be noted here is that the bride stayed with the guests in the same room. They were engaged in conversation whilst she was there waiting for them to go. Her husband, the Prophet, was too shy to indicate to them that they should leave, even though he went out and came back in, making it clear that he was not interested in what they were talking about, they remained oblivious to the fact that they were embarrassing the Prophet and his new wife. We know from other reports that most people had left, but three guests had stayed on as Anas describes. Whilst it might be suggested that the verse disapproves of what happened, the clear disapproval is only of those three people who had stayed on. The verse instructs people that when they visit the Prophet for a meal, they should leave when the meal is over. As for screening the Prophet's wives, this ruling applies only to them. It does not apply to any other woman. It is well known that special regulations applied to the Prophet's wives and these were not applicable to anyone else. The verse does not comment on the presence of men and women on this occasion, or indeed on any other.

On other occasions we see the bride serving the guests. When Abu Usayd al-Sāʿidī got married, he invited the Prophet and his companions. It was his wife, Umm Usayd [who was the bride according to Muslim's version] who cooked the food and served it. She had also the previous night soaked some dates with water in a stone pot. When the Prophet finished eating, she blended the dates with the water and gave it to him as a special treat. (Related by al-Bukhari and Muslim)

Al-Bukhari relates this hadith under the chapter heading: 'A woman undertaking to serve men herself at a wedding.' According to Ibn

Ḥajar, a woman may serve her husband and his guests. Needless to say, this applies when no misconduct is feared, and provided that the woman is dressed as Islām requires.

## Celebrating Eid

Another important feature that shows that the Muslim community during the Prophet's lifetime was a mixed society is his insistence that women should attend the Eid Prayer, which was offered at a wide, open area just outside Madinah. Anas ibn Mālik narrated: "When the Prophet settled in Madinah, he realized that its people had two annual festive occasions. He said to them: 'God has replaced these two days of yours with what is better: Eid *al-Fiṭr* and Eid *al-Aḍḥā.*'" (Related by al-Nasā'ī)

A hadith related by al-Bukhari quotes Ḥafṣah bint Sīrīn: "We used to prohibit our adolescent women from going out to prayer on the Eid occasions. A woman came to our place and resided in the palace of Bani Khalaf. She reported as regards her sister: 'My sister asked the Prophet whether a woman who had no top garment need not attend the Eid Prayer. He said: "Let her sister give her of her own garments, so that she will attend the goodness there and take part in the believers' prayer." When Umm 'Aṭiyyah arrived I asked her: 'Did you hear that from the Prophet?' She said: 'Yes, may my father be sacrificed for him – it was her practice to say this whenever she mentioned the Prophet – I heard him saying: "All young women and those who normally stay indoors and the ones having their periods should come to attend the goodness and take part in the believers' prayer. Those menstruating, however, should remain outside the praying area."'"" Ḥafṣah asked: "Even the women on their periods?" Umm 'Aṭiyyah said: "Do they not attend Arafat and other functions?"

Al-Bukhari enters this hadith in the chapter headed: 'Women having a period attend the Eid, take part in the supplication and stay apart from the prayer place.' Ibn Ḥajar explains what the Prophet meant by saying, "Let her sister give her of her own garments". This means her sister or neighbour should lend her a garment she does not need at the time. Others have suggested that it means that she shares her own garment with her. Still others say that this is given by way of exaggeration, meaning that women should come anyway, even if two are wearing one garment. It appears that people stopped adolescent girls from attending the Eid Prayer because practices and values changed after the early period of Islam. The hadith quoting Umm 'Aṭiyyah explains the reason behind the ruling: women should attend this blessed occasion and share in the Muslims' supplication.

The Prophet's companions did not appear to take into account the change in values and deterioration in morality after the early period. They continued to give the same ruling as was current during the Prophet's lifetime. Umm 'Aṭiyyah gave this hadith and its ruling a long time after the Prophet's death, and none of his companions has given a different ruling. Hence, the Prophet's ruling and his companions' practice remain valid for all time.

We mention the hadiths speaking of the Eid Prayer in the context of joyous occasions and public celebrations because the Eid Prayer is not merely a prayer followed by a sermon; it is a social occasion. It is held outside the city so that it can be attended by the largest possible number of people. Moreover, had the prayer been the main function, the Prophet would not have asked anyone who could not pray, such as menstruating women, to attend. Yet he insisted that they should attend, take part in God's glorification, declare their commitment to Islam, and participate in the supplication. He wanted all to come, old and young, adult and child, male and female, including those who could not pray. Even a woman who did not have an outer garment to wear could borrow one. This is certainly more than a mere worship occasion; it is a social occasion in which all take part.

‘Ā’ishah narrated: “Abu Bakr came in when I had two of the Anṣār’s maids. Both were singing some poetry of what the Anṣār composed after the Battle of Bu‘āth. They were not good singers. [In another version they are said to have also played the tambourine to accompany their singing.] Abu Bakr chided them, saying: ‘Are the devil’s instruments to be played in God’s Messenger’s home?’ The Prophet said: ‘Abu Bakr! Every community has a day of festivity, and this is ours.’” (Related by al-Bukhari and Muslim)

What we learn from this hadith is that the Prophet sanctioned the singing in his own home by two maids and listened to it. Although they were not professional singers, it was clear that they were singing and using a musical instrument which Abu Bakr called a ‘devil’s instrument.’ However, the Prophet explained to Abu Bakr that on such a joyous occasion people needed to have some fun, as long as it did not go against Islamic values. The two maids were singing poetic verses that were compiled after a battle that took place more than three years before the Prophet and his companions migrated to Madinah. The warring parties were the two Arab tribes in Madinah, the Aws and the Khazraj, who were to become the Anṣār. Thus, the singing was of the type that extolled the bravery of fighters and the virtue of defending one’s people even if that meant sacrificing one’s own life. Had the two maids’ songs been of the erotic type that described women’s beauty or encouraged drinking, the Prophet would not have allowed them to proceed. He so intervened on other occasions when any singer stepped over the line of what was acceptable in Islam.

Imam Ibn Hajar mentions in his commentary that this hadith indicates the permissibility of listening to a woman’s singing, even if she is unrelated to the one who is listening. The Prophet did not censure Abu Bakr for listening to the singing, but he censured Abu Bakr’s rebuke of the singers. They, in fact, continued to sing, with the Prophet and Abu Bakr in the room until ‘Ā’ishah had had enough and signalled them to leave.

The occasion when a number of Abyssinians celebrated with folk dancing in the Prophet's mosque in Madinah is often mentioned when scholars speak about the role of the mosque in the life of the Muslim community. It is also cited when scholars speak about what is permissible for women in the mosque, because 'Ā'ishah attended on that occasion.

'Ā'ishah narrated: "It was the Eid occasion, and people from those parts normally played with spears and shields. Either I asked the Prophet or he said to me, 'Would you like to look at them?' I said that I would. He placed me behind him, and I put my cheek on his cheek. He said to them: 'Let us see what you do.' When I had had enough the Prophet asked me: 'Is this enough for you?' I answered that it was, and he told me to go." (Related by al-Bukhari and Muslim) In another version, 'Ā'ishah says that 'Umar reproached them, but the Prophet stopped him and told them that they need not be worried.

Ibn Ḥajar said: "The hadith makes it clear that permissible entertainment is allowed. It also tells of the Prophet's fine manners with his family... That 'Ā'ishah said that the Prophet was covering her with his garment indicates that this was after the obligation placed on the Prophet's wives to remain behind a screen. It also tells us that it is permissible for women to look at men. Some scholars who say that this is not permissible claim that 'Ā'ishah was still young at the time. Yet it appears that this occurred after she had attained maturity. It is clear that this took place when the Abyssinian delegation came to Madinah, which was in Year 7, and she was at least 15 years old at the time. *Qadi* 'Iyāḍ said that the hadith shows that it is permissible for women to look at what men are doing. What is discouraged is for them to enjoy looking at tempting aspects.

What we see portrayed in this incident with the Abyssinians playing in the mosque on Eid Day gives a strong indication that provides chances for the marking of this festive occasion with decent entertainment. Women may certainly attend such activities and enjoy the shows that may be presented. We must also suppose that other women, of all ages, watched the fun that was presented. For if 'Ā'ishah watched them from behind the Prophet, with a number of his companions present, it stands to reason that other women must have heard of what was going on in the mosque and also came to watch and enjoy the scene, just like 'Ā'ishah did. After all, Muslim women used to go to the mosque at all times of the day and night, for no less than 12 different purposes as already discussed. Besides, the mosque provided a clean environment and ample space where Muslims looked after their various affairs.

It is true that 'Ā'ishah stood behind the Prophet when she watched, and he covered her with his robes, but then this was required of the Prophet's wives, as part of their special status. Other Muslim women needed only to observe normal Islamic standards that apply to meeting with men. We stress that Islam must be taken as a whole and not piecemeal. While Islam encourages women to attend good occasions and celebrations, it also commands its followers to dress in a decent manner, lowering one's gaze and avoiding areas of congestion. Its aim is to provide an atmosphere of purity and morality. All this applies to the mosque in as much as it applies to a lecture theatre and a public square.

Imam al-Nawawī, who wrote a full commentary on Muslim's anthology of authentic hadiths, comments on the Prophet's insistence on all women attending the Eid Prayer: "The Prophet said that the purpose is that they may 'attend the goodness and take part in the believers' prayer.' This means that Islam encourages people, men and women, to attend gatherings which include good things where those in attendance join in a supplication to God, or devote themselves to the glorification of God, or study groups." This means that Islam encourages women's participation in marking good occasions, provided that Islamic standards of morality and propriety are observed. Such occasions include, in our view, attending military parades which demonstrate the strength of a Muslim country. Such a parade should be within the framework defined by the Qur'anic verse that requires the Muslim community to "Make ready against them whatever force you can muster." (8: 60) Likewise, sporting competitions may be included in good gatherings, as these demonstrate physical strength.

Salamah ibn al-Akwaʿ, a companion of the Prophet, narrated: "The Prophet passed by a group from the Aslam clan of the Anṣār, who were having an archery match. He said to them: 'Go on and aim your arches, you descendants of Ishmael. I am with this group.' The other group held their archers and stopped aiming them. The Prophet asked them why have they stopped. They said: 'How can we when you are with the others?' He said: 'Then continue; I am with both your groups.'" (Related by al-Bukhari)

During the Prophet's lifetime, horse racing was a sport people enjoyed, but under Islam, this sport is not associated with betting as it is today in most countries and as it was in Arabia in pre-Islamic days. The practice in the early days of Islam was that horses prepared for such a sport would be kept slim and not be allowed to be overweight. They thus remain fitter and faster. ʿAbdullāh ibn ʿUmar narrated: "The Prophet organised a race between horses that were kept slim, starting from al-Ḥafyā' making their finishing line at Thaniyyat al-Wadāʿ, with the distance being around six or seven miles. He also organised a race between horses that were not kept slim, with the starting line at Thaniyyat al-Wadāʿ and the finishing line at the Mosque of the Zurayq clan. The distance was a mile or so." Ibn ʿUmar was one of the participants in that race. (Related by al-Bukhari and Muslim)

## Enquiring after Others

In Islamic society men and women may enquire after one another when they meet, whether such a meeting is accidental or planned. In the story about Moses' flight from Egypt and his arrival in Madyan, the Qur'anic account includes the following: "When he arrived at the wells of Madyan, he found there a large group of people drawing water [for their herds and flocks], and at some distance from them he found two women who were keeping back their flock. He asked them: 'What is the matter with you two?' They said: 'We cannot water [our animals] until the herdsmen drive home. Our father is a very old man.' So he watered their flock for them, and then he withdrew into the shade and prayed: 'My Lord! Truly am I in dire need of any good which You may send me.'" (28: 23-24)

So we see the Prophet Moses speaking to the two young ladies who were total strangers to him, enquiring about their situation and offering help. Although this occurred before he became a prophet, had there been anything wrong or unacceptable in this situation, God would have pointed to it in the Qur'anic account.

We may also quote here the authentic hadith that says: "The Prophet established a bond of brotherhood between Salmān and Abu al-Dardā'. Once Salmān went to visit Abu al-Dardā' and saw his wife wearing plain clothes. He asked her the reason and she told him: 'Your brother, Abu al-Dardā', does not care for anything in this life.'" (Related by al-Bukhari)

Ibn Ḥajar says of this hadith: "It includes several points such as the commendable practices of establishing a bond of brotherhood dedicated to God's service, visiting friends and brothers, speaking to a woman who is unrelated to us, enquiring about something in order to correct a wrong situation, even though it is apparently of no direct concern to the person making the enquiry."

We may add here that the Prophet has taught us to offer the Islamic greeting of peace to anyone we meet, whether they are known to us or total strangers. From such texts as we have quoted, we learn that such greetings should be accompanied by enquiring after other people, particularly when we see something that may call for our help.

## During social visits

Men and women may also meet when a man goes home to find that some women are visiting his wife. Umm Salamah, the Prophet's wife, reports: "I once heard the Prophet advising against offering voluntary prayers after one has offered the obligatory prayer of 'Aṣr. I later saw him offering these two *rak'ahs* after he had prayed 'Aṣr. He then entered my home when I had some women from the Ḥarām clan of the Anṣār visiting me..." (Related by al-Bukhari and Muslim)

What is relevant to our discussion is the part stating that the Prophet went in when his wife, Umm Salamah, was entertaining female visitors. This means that it is perfectly legitimate for a Muslim woman to visit a female friend when her husband is at home. The hadith continues to mention that Umm Salamah asked the Prophet about his voluntary prayer after 'Aṣr when he had spoken against such. He explained that on that particular occasion, he was offering two *rak'ahs* in lieu of those he habitually offered after Ẓuhr but could not do so on that particular day.

Focusing on the same point of men and women meeting together on social visits and speaking to each other, we may quote the following hadiths:

'Ā'ishah narrated: "The Prophet came into my home when I had a Jewish woman visiting me. The woman said to me: 'Do you realize that you will be tested when you are in your graves?' The Prophet was disturbed. He said: 'Only the Jews will be tested.' A few days later, the Prophet said to me: 'Do you realize that it has been revealed to me that you will be tested in the graves?' After that, I heard the Prophet often appealing to God for protection against torment in the grave." (Related by al-Bukhari and Muslim)

Abu Mūsā al-Ash'ari reports: "...Asmā' bint 'Umays, who came with us, went to visit Ḥafṣah, the Prophet's wife. Asmā' had been among those who had migrated to Abyssinia. 'Umar came in to see Ḥafṣah, his daughter, when Asmā' was with her. He asked who she was and Ḥafṣah answered: 'She is Asmā' bint 'Umays.' He said: 'Is this the Abyssinian woman? Is this the seafarer?' Asmā' answered: 'Yes'..." (Related by al-Bukhari and Muslim)

'Abdullāh ibn 'Amr ibn al-'Āṣ narrated: "A group from the clan of Hāshim went to see Asmā' bint 'Umays. Then Abu Bakr, her husband, came in and saw them. He did not like this and mentioned the fact to the Prophet, adding however: 'I have seen nothing untoward.' The Prophet said: 'God has preserved her from anything like that.' The Prophet then stood on the platform and said: 'Let no man enter the home of a woman who is on her own unless he is accompanied by one or two people.'" (Related by Muslim)

Qays ibn Abi Ḥāzim reports: "Abu Bakr went into the place of a woman from the tribe of Aḥmus, called Zaynab bint al-Muhājir. He noticed that she did not say a word. He asked why she did not speak. They told him that she had vowed to offer the pilgrimage keeping silent and saying not a word. He said to her: 'Speak. This is unlawful for you. This is a practice that belongs to the days of ignorance.' She spoke and asked him who he was. He said: 'I am a man from the Muhājirīn.' She asked: 'Of which Muhājirīn?' He said: 'From the Quraysh.' She again asked: 'From which of the Quraysh clans?' He said: 'You are certainly inquisitive. I am Abu Bakr.' She asked him:

'How long will we continue to follow this good path shown to us by God Almighty after we had been in ignorance?' He said: 'You will continue to follow it, as long as your leaders remain faithful to it.' She said: 'Who are the leaders?' He said: 'Are there not among your people some notables who are obeyed when they give orders?' She said: 'Yes.' He said: 'These are the leaders." (Related by al-Bukhari)

## More Than Mere Conversation

Numerous hadiths speak of the Prophet visiting women and talking to them about whatever might have been of concern to them. Other people might have been in the house. Yet at no time was the Prophet with a woman alone behind closed doors. Arabs often did not have what we would now call a front door. Hence, the reports speaking of someone visiting another often say: 'This person entered our place...' This is the reason for the Qur'anic instructions that people should first seek permission before entering a home other than their own.[5]

'Ā'ishah narrated: "Hālah bint Khuwaylid, Khadījah's sister, sought permission to enter the Prophet's home. He recognized Khadījah's way of seeking permission. He said: 'My Lord, let it be Hālah.' I felt jealous and said: 'Why do you speak of an elderly Quraysh woman who lost her teeth and died many years ago, when God has given you one who is better?' (Related by al-Bukhari and Muslim)

Jābir ibn 'Abdullāh narrated that the Prophet said to Asmā' bint 'Umays: "Why are my brother's children so thin? [He meant Ja'far ibn Abu Ṭālib's children.] Are they in poverty?" She said: "No, but the evil eye may affect them." He said: "Supplicate for them." She read out [her supplication] to him and he said: "Supplicate for them."

5. Thus, on reaching the door way, a visitor would stop, say a greeting aloud, identify himself and request permission to enter.

Anas said that the Prophet did not enter any home other than his wives' homes except Umm Sulaym's. He was asked about this and he said: "I feel for her as her brother was killed fighting with me." (Related by al-Bukhari and Muslim) An explanation is given in Ibn Ḥajar's *Fatḥ al-Bārī*, quoting al-Ḥumaydī: "Perhaps he meant regularly." Ibn al-Tīn said that he meant he visited Umm Sulaym frequently.

Anas narrated: "The Prophet visited us when there were only myself, my mother and my aunt, Umm Ḥarām. He said: 'Let us pray together.' [It was not a time for obligatory prayer.] He led us in a congregational prayer, and afterwards he prayed for us all in my mother's household, appealing to God to give us of every good thing in this life and in the life to come." (Related by Muslim)

Other hadiths bear examples of the very high standard of tender care extended between men and women, including help in personal hygiene. Anas ibn Mālik narrated: "The Prophet used to visit Umm Ḥarām bint Milḥān, [Anas's aunt,] and she used to serve him with food. Umm Ḥarām was married to 'Ubādah ibn al-Ṣāmit. One day the Prophet visited her and she gave him a meal. Then she examined his head to pick out any insect that might be there. The Prophet then had a nap. When he woke up, he smiled. She asked him what caused his smile. He said: 'I saw in my dream groups of my followers on a military expedition to serve God's cause, riding in the sea and looking like kings on their thrones.'" (Related by al-Bukhari and Muslim)

Commenting on this hadith, Imam Ibn Ḥajar says: "This hadith indicates that it is appropriate for a woman to serve a guest, who is unrelated to her, giving him food and preparing things for his comfort... It also shows that it is appropriate for her to help with examining his head to rid him of insects... This appeared problematic for some scholars. Ibn 'Abd al-Barr said that he thought that either

Umm Ḥarām or her sister, Umm Sulaym, breast-fed the Prophet, which meant that each of them was either his mother or aunt through breast-feeding. This would explain why the Prophet sometimes had a nap at her place and she helped him with something only very close relatives, i.e. *maḥram*, could do. Other scholars said that the Prophet was immune to sin. He was in full control of his desires, even in relation to his wives. This, then, applies in even greater degrees to his relations with other women. He was known to never have committed any indecent deed. Thus, we can say that such contact was permitted to him as a special concession applying to him only. He then added that such visits and contacts might have occurred before women were ordered to observe the Islamic dress code. This, however, is refuted by the fact that this took place during the Prophet's Farewell Pilgrimage, long after the order to observe the dress code. As for its being a special concession granted the Prophet, 'Iyāḍ objects to this saying that such a special concession can only be confirmed by a text, but in this case we have none. That the Prophet was immune to sin is certain, but the normal situation is that we need evidence before we can say of anything the Prophet did that it applied to him only. Otherwise, whatever he did applies to all, and we can follow his example without hesitation. Al-Dumyāṭī strongly refutes the claim that Umm Ḥarām and Umm Sulaym were closely related to the Prophet. He says that anyone who suggests this is totally mistaken, whether he claims this was through blood relation or through breast-feeding because the Prophet's mothers are well known and those who breast-fed him are also well known. Ibn Ḥajar concludes that he prefers the argument that this was a special concession given to the Prophet, and that it cannot be refuted on the basis of the absence of evidence, because the evidence is clear for all to see, but God knows best.

In a ruling which he expressed on Qatar television and I have in writing, Dr Yusuf al-Qaradawi says: "I cannot see any trace of evidence, clear or implied, to support the claim that it was a special concession applicable to the Prophet only."

We may add that Ibn Ḥajar himself gives us further evidence that such hadiths speaking of close personal care between men and women who are unrelated are applicable generally and are not specific to the Prophet. This he gives in commenting on the next hadith related by Abu Mūsā al-Ash'arī who mentions how a woman of his clan, married to one of his brothers, examined his head to pick out any lice or little insects. This took place as Abu Mūsā arrived in Makkah, joining the Prophet and his companions on their pilgrimage.

Abu Mūsā narrated: "The Prophet sent me on a mission to Yemen. I came back and joined him at al-Baṭḥā' [in Makkah]. He asked me how I intended my pilgrimage to be conducted. I said: 'I made my intention as the Prophet intended his pilgrimage.' He asked me whether I brought my sacrifice with me. I told him I had not. He instructed me to do the *ṭawāf* around the Ka'bah and the *sa'ī* between the two hills of al-Safa and al-Marwah. He also instructed me to release myself from consecration, or *iḥrām*. I then went to a woman from my clan who combed my hair, or perhaps washed my head." (Related by al-Bukhari and Muslim) In another version of this hadith the last sentence reads: "I then went to one of the women of the Qays clan who deloused my head."

Ibn Ḥajar comments concerning the identity of the woman involved: "What appears at first sight is that she belonged to the tribe of Qays 'Aylān, but these are unrelated to the Ash'arīs. However, the second version of the hadith suggests that 'the Qays clan' in this instance refers to Qays ibn Sulaym, Abu Mūsā's father, which means that the woman was married to one of his brothers: either Abu Ruham, Abu Burdah or perhaps Muhammad."

What we can conclude is that close contact and personal care that requires physical proximity and perhaps physical contact is allowed when there is no possibility of temptation. As clearly appears from the texts we have, such immunity to temptation occurs only in certain conditions in special social circumstances. This suggests that a long association between devout believers may bring about sublime feelings that leave no room for sexual desire. Such sublime feelings cannot prevail except through long association. Examples of such long association are found in the early Muslim community. One of these is the brother-sister relation between the Prophet and Umm Sulaym and Umm Ḥarām. Another is the mother-son relation between Sahlah bint Suhayl, Abu Hudhayfah's wife, and Sālim, his servant. With such relations, the sexual attraction almost disappears. Besides, we think that this is indicated in the Qur'anic verse that lists the men before whom a woman may appear without a head covering. This list names a woman's very close relatives and adds: "such male attendants as are free of physical desire." (24: 31) Freedom from physical desire is a result of long association. Old age weakens such desire but does not free a person of it completely.

## Different Purposes of Interaction

A number of hadiths speak of social visits and other forms of interaction between men and women during the Prophet's lifetime. The Prophet himself was party to such interaction, as clearly appears in the following hadiths. Anas reports: "The Prophet saw women and children coming from a wedding. He stood up and went to meet them. He said to them, repeating his words three times: 'You are of the ones I love most.'" (Related by al-Bukhari and Muslim)

'Ā'ishah narrated: "Hind bint 'Utbah came to us and said to the Prophet: 'Messenger of God! There was time when I loved no household to be more humiliated than yours. Now there is no household I love to see in a more honourable position than yours.' He said: 'And I, by the One Who holds my soul in His hand...'" (Related by al-Bukhari and Muslim) His words, 'and I', mean that he wished her the same after having been aggrieved by her action a few years earlier, when she arranged for a man to kill his uncle, Ḥamzah, and then went on herself to disfigure him.

Another hadith narrated by 'Ā'ishah mentions that she borrowed a necklace from her sister Asmā', and it was lost. The Prophet sent some of his companions to look for it. It was time for prayer and they offered their prayer without having ablution. When they came back they complained to the Prophet. A Qur'anic verse was then revealed to allow dry ablution, or *tayammum*. Usayd ibn Ḥuḍayr said to the Prophet: "May God reward you well. Whatever adverse situation you encounter, God gives you a way out of it together with blessings for all Muslims." (Related by al-Bukhari and Muslim) Dry ablution is allowed in place of normal *wudu* in a scenario where the person does not have access to water, or has only a small amount which he needs for drinking, or in the case of an illness or injury that prevents the use of water. Usayd's comment refers to the fact that Islam provides concessions to deal with any adverse situation or difficulty.

This last hadith does not speak of direct contact between the Prophet and any woman, but it is relevant to our discussion because the lost necklace belonged to the Prophet's sister-in-law and the Prophet sent some of his companions who were unrelated to her to look for it.

Women came to the Prophet requesting him to pray for them or their families. 'Aṭā' ibn Rabāḥ reports that 'Abdullāh ibn 'Abbās asked him if he would like to see a woman who will definitely be in heaven? 'Aṭā' said that he was interested to see her. 'Abdullāh ibn 'Abbās said: "It is this black woman. She came to the Prophet requesting him to pray for her as she suffered from epilepsy and she might be exposed when she had a fit. The Prophet said to her: 'If you wish you can bear your affliction with patience and you will be in heaven, or I will pray to God for you to be cured.' She said: 'I will bear it with patience, but pray for me that I may not be exposed during a fit.' He prayed for her." (Related by al-Bukhari and Muslim)

Anas reports on one of the Prophet's visits to his (Anas's) mother, Umm Sulaym: "He prayed for Umm Sulaym and the people in her household. Umm Sulaym then said to him: 'Messenger of God! I have a small request.' He asked her what that was. She said: 'Your servant, Anas.' He prayed for me mentioning every good thing in this life and the life to come and said: 'My Lord, grant him wealth and children, and bless him.' I am now one of the wealthiest people among the Anṣār. My daughter Umaynah tells me that when al-Ḥajjāj arrived in Basrah, more than 120 of my offspring had already been dead." (Related by al-Bukhari and Muslim) It should be added that Anas was saying this at a time when he was already well into his eighties. Most of those he refers to of his offspring had died during a plague epidemic.

Muslim women used to come to the Prophet requesting him to pray for them or their children and families. They knew that a prayer offered by the Prophet was certain to be answered. He would oblige anyone who requested him for prayer in the best way that suited the occasion. Asmā' bint Abu Bakr narrated that she was in an advanced stage of pregnancy when she travelled from Makkah when the Muslims migrated to Madinah. She says: "I left when my pregnancy was almost in full term. As I arrived in Madinah, I stopped at Qubā' and gave birth there [to my son 'Abdullāh]. I took him to the Prophet and he placed him on his lap. He asked someone to bring him a date and he chewed it, then he put a drop of his saliva in the child's mouth. Thus the first thing that went inside 'Abdullāh's body was the Prophet's saliva. Then he placed the date in his mouth and rubbed his gums with it, and prayed for him and blessed him. He was the first child to be born in the Islamic period." (Related by al-Bukhari and Muslim)

## Host and guest

It is a universal human practice that when a person wants to honour others or show them good will, he invites them to a meal. The Prophet advised us that when we receive an invitation we should accept it as long as that is feasible. The Prophet accepted invitations from his companions, even when he knew they could only serve him with very simple food. In fact, he valued even the most simple of foods and never looked with disdain on any. If he did not like something, he simply did not eat of it.

Anas reports: "The Prophet had a Persian neighbour who was known for his fine cooking. He cooked something for the Prophet and then came over to invite him. The Prophet pointed to 'Ā'ishah and asked the man: 'What about this one?' [He wanted to know whether the invitation was for both of them.] The man said: 'No.' So, the Prophet said: 'No.' The man came back later, renewing his invitation, but the Prophet again asked him: 'What about this one?' The man said: 'No.' So the Prophet said: 'No.' Once more the man came back inviting the Prophet, and once more the Prophet asked him: 'What about this one?' On this third occasion, the man said: 'Yes.' Both rose and went quickly to his home." (Related by Muslim)

Anas ibn Mālik reports that his grandmother Mulaykah invited the Prophet after having cooked something. "He (the Prophet) came over and ate of her food. He then said: 'Get ready so that I can lead you in prayer.' I took out a straw mat which was used so much that it became black and I sprayed it with water. The Prophet stood up and I formed a row with an orphan behind him, and the old woman stood behind us. He prayed two *rak'ahs* and then left." (Related by al-Bukhari and Muslim)

In commenting on this hadith, Imam Ibn Ḥajar says that this hadith makes clear that accepting an invitation is strongly recommended, even if it is not for a wedding and the host is a woman, provided that we are certain that no temptation to sin can occur.

Fāṭimah bint Qays reports on the arrangements the Prophet suggested to her with regard to where to spend her waiting period after she had been divorced for the third and last time. He first told her to stay with Umm Sharīk, but then thought better of the situation and said to her: "She is a woman who is frequently visited by my companions." Another version mentions: "...The Prophet told me to move to Umm Sharīk's home. I said that I would do so. He then changed his mind and said to me: 'Do not do that. Umm Sharīk receives numerous guests.'" (Related by Muslim)

We may also add here a report that is not included in either of the two *Ṣaḥīḥ* anthologies. It confirms that it is appropriate for women to receive male guests in the absence of their husbands, if other women are present, provided that these guests are known to the husbands and trusted by them. Al-Ṭabarī relates from Qatādah: "The Prophet specified (in the conditions of the pledge of allegiance given by women) that they would not wail for their dead relatives, and that they would not talk to men. 'Abd al-Raḥmān ibn 'Awf said: 'We may have guests and we may be away from our women.' The Prophet said: 'I do not mean those.'"

What we should stress here is that interaction between a woman and her male guests is permissible, provided always that she is not in complete privacy, alone with one man behind closed doors, and that her guests are known to, and trusted by her husband or her father if she is unmarried. More rigid restrictions that do not allow interaction between men and women are often imposed by social tradition rather than Islamic legislation.

## Exchanging Gifts

When we speak of social interaction between men and women, the exchange of gifts is a point to consider. In short, is it permissible for men and women to give gifts to each other? Before we cite any hadith in evidence we need to remember that Islam takes a very serious approach to morality and expects its followers to observe its moral code. This means that a gift must never be intended to gain any special privilege. It must never be given in support of a claim or in the hope of achieving any gain. In other words, a gift should be intended purely for cementing social relations, with the expectation of no reward other than the one that comes from God. Bearing this in mind we may look at the following hadiths which speak of gifts exchanged between men and women, including the Prophet who gave gifts to women and received gifts from others. In neither case were the women concerned related to him.

ʿĀ'ishah narrated: "I never begrudged any woman's position with the Prophet as I begrudged Khadījah, even though she died before he married me. I was jealous of her because I often heard him mentioning her. God ordered him to give her the news that a lofty home-made of hollowed pearls will be her abode in heaven. The Prophet used to slaughter a sheep and send generous gifts of its meat to women who were her intimate friends." (Related by al-Bukhari and Muslim)

In a narration from Sahl ibn Saʿd: "A woman brought a *burdah* to the Prophet. Do you know what a *burdah* is like?" They said: "Yes, it is a large piece of cloth with embroidered ends, used to cover oneself with." "As she gave it to him, she said: 'Messenger of God! I embroidered this with my own hand to gift it to you.' The Prophet took it from her, and it was obvious that he needed it. He then came out to us using it as his upper garment. A man who was sitting with us said to the Prophet: 'Messenger of God! Give it to me as a gift.' The Prophet said: 'I will.' He sat with us for a while then he went home and folded it up. He sent it to the man. People said to the man: 'You have not done well by asking him to give it to you, as you know he never refuses a request.' The man said: 'By God, I only wanted it so that it will be the cloth I will be wrapped in when I die.' It was indeed his shroud with which he was buried." (Related by al-Bukhari)

Anas ibn Mālik tells us about a gift his mother sent to the Prophet after one of his weddings: "When the Prophet had his wedding to Zaynab, Umm Sulaym said to me: 'Would it not be good if we sent a gift to the Prophet?' I said: 'Yes, indeed.' She got some dates, ghee and dried milk and made *ḥaysah* [a dish that blends all three ingredients until they are a consistent mixture] in a pot. She told me to take it to him." Muslim's version is more detailed as Anas says that his mother said: "Anas, take this to God's Messenger and say to him: My mother has sent you this and she gives you her greeting and says that this is too little from us." "I did as she told me. The Prophet said to me: 'Place this here.' He then told me to invite certain men he named, adding, 'Invite also whoever you meet.'" (Related by al-Bukhari and Muslim)

Umm al-Faḍl bint al-Ḥārith mentions that some men were with her on the day of attendance at Arafat during the pilgrimage. Some said that the Prophet was fasting, while others said he was not. She sent him a glass of milk as he was on his camel, not moving. He took the glass of milk and drank it. (Related by al-Bukhari and Muslim) Ibn Ḥajar comments that this hadith clearly indicates that it is perfectly appropriate for a man to accept a gift from a woman.

## When Visiting Sick People

Another aspect of social interaction concerns visiting those who are ill. The question that is relevant to our theme is whether it is permissible for women to visit sick men or for men to visit women who are sick. Al-Bukhari relates the following hadith under the chapter heading: 'Women visiting sick men', adding that Umm al-Dardā' visited a man from the Anṣār. Said 'Ā'ishah: "When God's Messenger arrived in Madinah, both Abu Bakr and Bilāl were taken ill. I visited them and said: Father, how are you feeling? Bilāl, how are you feeling? When Abu Bakr was troubled by fever, he would chant:

> 'Each one is greeted with "Good Morning" by members
> of his family, yet death may overtake him at any moment.'

When Bilāl felt a little refreshed, he would chant:

> 'I wonder whether I would ever spend a night in the Valley of Makkah, surrounded by its wild plants, some strong and some weak!
> Would I ever see the springs at Mijannah? Would I ever set sight at the two mountains, Shāmah and Ṭafīl?'

I went to God's Messenger and told him all this. He prayed: 'My Lord! Make Madinah as dear to us as Makkah, or even dearer. Make it a healthy place for us, and bless for us its measures. Remove its fever and place it at al-Juḥfah.'"[6] (Related by al-Bukhari)

In his commentary on this hadith, Ibn Ḥajar says: "The fact that al-Bukhari gives a sub-heading specifying women visiting sick men implies that the visitors and those who are visited are unrelated. In such a visit the recognized conditions of decency and propriety must be observed." He also says: "... Some scholars have pointed out that this was certainly before women were ordered to observe the Islamic dress code. Their point is answered by scholars who say that this is irrelevant, because it is permissible for a woman to visit a man who is sick, provided that she observes the Islamic dress code. What applies to both situations is the condition of propriety."

Here is another hadith confirming the permissibility of such visits: Umm Mubashshir bint al-Barā' ibn Ma'rūr went to see Ka'b ibn Malik shortly before his death. She said to him: "Abu 'Abd al-Raḥmān! Give my greetings to my son." He said: "May God forgive you, Umm Mubashshir! Have you not heard what the Prophet said: 'A Muslim's spirit is a bird on the trees of heaven. God returns it to his body on

6. Al-Juhfah is a place to the South-West of Madinah, near the Red Sea. It was very thinly populated and later became deserted. The Prophet's supplication meant that when the fever is placed there it would not become an epidemic.

the Day of Judgement.'" She said: "That is true. I pray to God for forgiveness."

This is a situation where we see a female companion of the Prophet visiting a man who is unrelated to her and speaking to him on his deathbed. The man was also a companion of the Prophet who fought many battles with him.

## Men Visiting Sick Women

'Ā'ishah narrated: "The Prophet went to see Ḍubā'ah bint al-Zubayr. He said to her: 'Perhaps you want to go on pilgrimage?' She said: 'I am in pain.' He said: 'You can start your pilgrimage, making a condition by saying: My Lord! I have a proviso that I release myself from consecration, or *iḥrām*, wherever I cannot proceed further.' She was married to al-Miqdād ibn al-Aswad." (Related by al-Bukhari and Muslim) Ḍubā'ah was the Prophet's cousin, as her father was al-Zubayr ibn 'Abd al-Muṭṭalib.

Jābir ibn 'Abdullāh reports that God's Messenger visited Umm al-Sā'ib, [or she was Umm al-Musayyib]. He said to her: "Why are you trembling, Umm al-Sā'ib?" She said: "It is because of my accursed fever." He said: "Do not curse fever, because it wipes away people's sins, just like the bellows of the ironmonger blows away foreign objects." (Related by Muslim)

This hadith reminds us of another related by Abu Dāwūd quoting Umm al-'Alā': "God's Messenger visited me during my illness. He said to me: 'Rejoice, Umm al-'Alā', for illness is an occasion when God removes from Muslims their sins, just like fire separates foreign objects from gold and silver.'" Al-Nasā'ī relates on the authority of Abu Umāmah: "A woman from the high land fell ill. The Prophet was the best visitor to this and any patient. He then said to her people: 'Should she die, let me know.'" Needless to say, the Prophet wanted to know so that he could attend her funeral and offer the *Janāzah* Prayer [i.e. prayer for a deceased person].

Abu Mulaykah narrated: "'Abdullāh ibn 'Abbās sought admission to visit 'Ā'ishah when she was very ill. She said: 'I fear that he would praise me!' People said to her: 'He is the Prophet's cousin and a distinguished figure in the Muslim community.' She told them to admit him. He asked her how she felt. She said: 'I am well, if I remain God-fearing.' He said: 'Then you are well, God willing. You are God's Messenger's wife, and the only one of his wives who never married before him. Your innocence was confirmed from on high.'" (Related by al-Bukhari) His last comment referred to the fact that when the false accusation was levelled at 'Ā'ishah, God declared her innocence in the Qur'an, with the relevant verses 24: 11-20.

So far, we have quoted texts that show that visiting the sick is a common practice in the Muslim community. What is more is that the quoted texts show that men used to visit sick women and women visited sick men. Another aspect of such mixing between men and women is that men visited their sick brethren in the presence of their female relatives. This was a clear mixed occasion when men and women were together.

'Abdullāh ibn 'Umar narrated: "Sa'd ibn 'Ubādah was taken ill. The Prophet visited him accompanied by 'Abd al-Raḥmān ibn 'Awf, Sa'd ibn Abi Waqqāṣ and 'Abdullāh ibn Mas'ūd. When he entered, he found him surrounded by his women folk. He asked whether he had passed away. They said: 'No, Messenger of God!' The Prophet was tearful. When those around saw him weeping, they wept. He said: 'Listen to me! God does not punish anyone for weeping or feeling their grief. He punishes for what this [pointing to his tongue] may say, or He may bestow His mercy.'" (Related by al-Bukhari and Muslim)

A similar case is mentioned in a hadith related by Mālik in *Al-Muwaṭṭa'* and al-Nasā'ī in his *Sunan*: Jābir ibn 'Atīq narrated: "God's

Messenger went to visit 'Abdullāh ibn Thābit when he was ill. He found him overpowered by his illness. He spoke loudly to him, but 'Abdullāh did not reply. The Prophet said: 'We all belong to God, and to Him will we all return. We are bound to lose you, Abu al-Rabīʿ.' The women around cried and wept. Jābir told them to be quiet, but the Prophet told him to leave them alone, for when the sick man has got it, they must not cry. The Prophet was asked what he meant by 'has got it', and he said, 'when he has died.' The man's daughter said: 'By God! I had sincerely hoped that you would be a martyr. You have just completed your preparations for jihad.' The Prophet said: 'God will reward him according to what he had intended.'"

This hadith also reminds us of another related by al-Ṭabarānī on the authority of Qays ibn Abi Ḥāzim who reports: "We visited Abu Bakr during his illness. I saw there a white woman with both her hands painted. She was keeping flies away from him. She was Asmā' bint 'Umays."[7]

All these hadiths show that the Prophet and his companions visited their brethren when they were sick. The women in the sick person's household were present and they talked to their visitors. We also note that a visitor may give a description of a woman in the household, as Abu Ḥāzim described Asmā', both of whom were companions of the Prophet.

## Sharing a Dwelling Place

People often have to share homes. In our modern times, families have become small units and often live in small homes, particularly in large cities. In former times, extended families shared the same home. There are other situations where homes are shared, such as a family needing to let out rooms in order to bolster their income.

7. At that time, Asmā' was Abū Bakr's wife.

Such situations inevitably lead to social mixing between men and women. In fact, the Prophet himself had to share a home with others. He lived in his uncle's home from the time when he was an eight-year old child until he became an adult. When he migrated to Madinah, he first lived in Abu Ayyūb's home.

Abu Ayyūb mentioned that the Prophet occupied the ground floor while Abu Ayyūb and his wife lived on the first floor. One night Abu Ayyūb thought about this and said: "We are walking here on top and the Prophet is down there!" He told his family to move to the side. They slept that night next to the wall. In the morning Abu Ayyūb requested that the Prophet move to the top floor, but the Prophet said: "Downstairs is easier for me." Abu Ayyūb said: "I will never go on top when you are downstairs." The Prophet moved upstairs and Abu Ayyūb moved to the ground floor. He used to prepare food for the Prophet. When the Prophet had eaten and returned the plate, Abu Ayyūb would look for the place where the Prophet's fingers had touched the food and eat from there. (Related by Muslim)

The Muslims who migrated to Madinah had to live with their Anṣārī brethren in their homes for a period of time, which might have lasted for several years. Khārijah ibn Zayd ibn Thābit reports on the authority of Umm al-ʿAlā', a woman from the Anṣār who pledged allegiance to the Prophet, that she said: "When the Anṣār had a draw to decide where the Muhājirīn would live, ʿUthmān ibn Maẓʿūn was the one who had to live with us. Then when he fell ill, we nursed him until he died. We wrapped him to prepare him for burial." (Related by al-Bukhari)

The Anṣār were very hospitable and they endeavoured to make the Muhājriīn more than welcome. Anas reports: "When they came to Madinah, the Muhājirīn were welcomed by the Anṣār. ʿAbd al-Raḥmān ibn ʿAwf was hosted by Saʿd ibn al-Rabīʿ who said to him: 'I will give you half of my wealth and will give up one of my two wives for you to marry.'" (Related by al-Bukhari)

Fāṭimah bint Qays reports that Abu Ḥafṣ al-Makhzūmī divorced her three times... The Prophet sent a message to her not to precipitate a new marriage without consulting him. He told her to stay with Umm Sharīk [during her waiting period]. He then sent her another message, saying: "Umm Sharīk is frequently visited by the early Muhājirīn. Move to Ibn Umm Maktūm's home. As he is blind, he will not see you when you remove your head covering." She moved into his home... (Related by Muslim)

## Mixing at Meal Times

Abu Hurayrah narrated: "A man came to the Prophet, and he sent word to his wives[8] but they replied that they had nothing but water. The Prophet asked his companions: 'Who will be this man's host tonight?' A man from the Anṣār said: 'I will.' He took him home with him. When they arrived home, the man said to his wife: 'Be hospitable to the Prophet's guest.' She said: 'We have nothing but my children's dinner.' Her husband said: 'Prepare the food and light your oil-lamp, and put your children to sleep if they want a dinner.' She did as her husband instructed. Then when she served the food, she faked that she wanted to fix the oil-lamp, but she put it out. They pretended to their guest that they were eating with him, but they did not touch the food, going to sleep without eating anything. In the morning, the Anṣār man went to the Prophet who said to him: 'Last night, God smiled at, or was pleased with what you and your wife did.'" In the version related by Muslim, he said: "God was pleased with what you two did with your guest last night." Then the Qur'anic verse referring to the Anṣār was revealed saying: "They give them preference over themselves, even though they are in want. Those who are saved from their own greed are truly successful." (59: 9) (Related by al-Bukhari and Muslim)

8. Apparently, the Prophet wanted to make sure that the man would receive good hospitality that night, so he sent a word to his wives asking whether they could give the man his dinner. - Editor's note.

When we read hadiths about the Prophet's companions sharing a meal, we often imagine that it was shared by men only. Yet it is often the case that the text speaks of men and women sharing the food, as is specifically clear in the second version of the following hadith:

Anas ibn Malik narrated that Abu Ṭalḥah, his stepfather, told his wife Umm Sulaym, to cook some food for the Prophet personally. "She did so and sent me with it... The Prophet put his hand on it and said, 'In the name of God.' He then told me to bring in ten people. When they went in, the Prophet told them to say God's name and eat. They did so, then he told me to bring in ten more. He continued to do so until 80 people had eaten. The Prophet then ate together with those who were at home with him, leaving some food on the plate." Another version of this hadith says: "The Prophet then ate together with Abu Ṭalḥah, Umm Sulaym and Anas ibn Mālik. Some food remained, and we gave it as a gift to our neighbours." (Related by Muslim)

Shaykh Muhammad Shukri ibn Hasan of Ankara, the author of an annotation of Muslim's *Ṣaḥīḥ* anthology published in Istanbul writes: "Based on the Prophet's eating with Umm Sulaym, scholars consider it permissible for a woman to eat with a man who is a stranger to her... Her face and hands are not required to be covered. Hence, a stranger may look at her face and hands normally, provided that he does not look at her lustfully or contemplate her charms."

'Ā'ishah narrated: "A woman visited the Prophet. Some meat was served to him and he was giving her of it. I said to him: 'Messenger of God! Do not dip your hand in it.'[9] He said: ''Ā'ishah, this lady used to visit us during Khadījah's lifetime. To be true to old friendships is part of faith.'" (Related by al-Saraqusṭī)

9. 'Ā'ishah perhaps said this out of a feeling of jealousy, as she saw her husband, the Prophet, paying special attention to his old visitor.

Umm Hānī' narrated: "On the day Makkah fell to Islam, Fāṭimah came to the Prophet and sat to his left, while Umm Hānī' sat to his right. A maid came in carrying a jug containing a drink. She handed it to him. He drank then gave the jug to Umm Hānī' to drink..."

Umm 'Imārah bint Ka'b narrated that the Prophet visited her, and she served him some food. He said to her "Won't you eat?" She said, "I am fasting."

In *Al-Muwaṭṭa'* we read: Mālik was asked: "Can a woman eat with someone who is not a *maḥram* to her or with her servant?" Mālik answered: "There is no harm in this, provided that it is in the way normally acceptable for a woman to eat with men. She may also eat with her husband or brother when he is eating with other men."

## Mixing during Travel

Travelling inevitably creates situations where people meet and join together in some activities, particularly when large means of transport are used, such as boats and aeroplanes, or when people used to travel in caravans, as was the case at the advent of Islam. Abu Mūsā al-Ash'arī narrated: "We heard of the Prophet's migration when we were still in Yemen. So, we set out to join him... We took a boat but our boat landed us in Negus's land in Abyssinia... We then joined the Prophet when he had just fought the Battle of Khaybar... Asmā' bint 'Umays, who was among the people who came with us, visited Ḥafṣah, the Prophet's wife. Asmā' was one of the Prophet's companions who had migrated to Abyssinia..." (Related by al-Bukhari and Muslim)[10]

10. Asma' was the wife of Ja'far ibn Abi Ṭālib, the Muslims' spokesman when they were questioned by Negus about the reasons for their migration to his country. Abū Mūsā and his people had accepted Islam and they thought that they must join the Prophet in Madinah to give their support given the newly founded state was facing serious threats. When they landed in Abyssinia, they met Ja'far and his group who welcomed them and invited them to stay, the Prophet had in any case sent them there instructing them to stay.

Marwān and al-Miswar ibn Makhramah, both companions of the Prophet, narrated: "... Women came to the Prophet, migrating to join him. Umm Kulthūm bint 'Uqbah ibn Abi Mu'ayṭ was one of those who migrated. She had only recently attained puberty. Her people came over, asking the Prophet to send her back with them, but he refused..." (Related by al-Bukhari)

Anas reports that his mother, Umm Sulaym was pregnant. "The Prophet was away travelling and she was with him. When the Prophet returned to Madinah, he never entered at night. As the Prophet and his companions were close to Madinah, she was in labour. Abu Ṭalḥah [her husband] stayed with her there..." (Related by Muslim)

'Imrān ibn Ḥuṣayn reports: "The Prophet was once travelling when a woman from the Anṣār, riding a she-camel, was irritated and cursed her she-camel. Hearing this, the Prophet said: 'Take away whatever is carried on that she-camel and leave it alone, because she is accursed.' I can almost see that she-camel now walking around, and no one goes near her." (Related by Muslim)

'Adiy ibn Ḥātim narrated: "When I was sitting with the Prophet a man came to him and complained of his poverty. Then another man came to complain of bandits attacking travellers. He asked me whether I had been to al-Ḥīrah [a town that used to be in southern Iraq]. I said: 'I have not been there, but I was informed about it.' He said: 'If you live long, you will see a time when a woman will travel in her howdah from al-Ḥīrah until she performs her *ṭawāf* at the Ka'bah fearing no one other than God.' I thought 'what about those robbers from the Ṭayyi' tribe who have spread fear in the land?'... I have most certainly seen women travelling alone from al-Ḥīrah until they performed their *ṭawāf*, entertaining no fear from anyone other than God..." (Related by al-Bukhari)

In his commentary on this hadith, Ibn Ḥajar says in reference to the statement, 'until she performs her *ṭawāf* at the Ka'bah': Ahmad adds in a version with a different chain of transmission that the travelling woman 'having no protection extended by anyone.'

The expression about extending protection refers to the traditional Arabian practice of extending *jiwār* to a person or a group, which meant that the one who is extending it and his tribe are ready to defend that person or group against any attack. All Arabs normally respected such *jiwār* so as to maintain good relations with other tribes. This version of the ḥadīth by Ahmad emphasises that a woman travelling alone would not feel any need to have such protection as she crossed such a great distance in areas that were mostly desert.

Ibn Ḥajar says elsewhere in his commentary: "The hadith reported by 'Ā'ishah stating that 'The best and most attractive way of jihad is the pilgrimage,' indicates that a woman may travel for pilgrimage with someone whom she knows to be reliable, even though he may not be her husband or *maḥram*... The well-known view of the Shāfi'ī School makes it a condition that a woman must travel with her husband or *maḥram* relative or with a group of reliable women. According to one view, one other reliable woman is enough. A view endorsed by al-Karābīsī in *Al-Muhadhdhab* suggests that a woman may travel alone if her route is safe. All this applies only to travel to perform the duties of hajj and *'umrah*. Al-Qaffāl stands out rather strangely in applying this to all travel, and this is endorsed by al-Ruwayyānī even though he mentions that it is contrary to proper statements... Further evidence in support of the permissibility of a woman travelling with a group of reliable women when such travel is felt to be safe is found in the hadith confirming that ''Umar permitted the Prophet's wives to offer the pilgrimage.' 'Umar, 'Uthmān, 'Abd al-Raḥmān ibn 'Awf and the Prophet's wives all agreed to this, and none of the Prophet's companions objected to it. Anyone of the Prophet's wives who declined this, her attitude was based on a specific reason. She did not consider the company of a *maḥram* to be essential for the permissibility of her travel. An argument in support of the permissibility of a woman travelling alone in times of safety is based on the hadith reported by 'Adiy ibn Ḥātim, stating: 'A time will soon come when a woman will travel on her howdah from al-Ḥīrah without her husband for a companion...' Some scholars object to this view saying that the hadith only indicates that this will take place, but does not mention that it is permissible. Yet this objection is answered by scholars who say that the context is one of praise, confirming the blessings in life under Islam. Hence, it should be taken as indicating permissibility." Ibn Ḥajar concludes by saying: "The indications already mentioned endorse the view that it is permissible".

Ibn Daqīq al-'Īd comments on the hadith that says: "No woman who believes in God and the Last Day may travel the distance covered in a day's travel unless she is accompanied by a *maḥram* relative," by saying that the term 'woman' is general in its implication and applies to all women. Some Mālikī scholars maintain the view that it applies only to young women. Elderly women who normally do not attract men may, according to them, travel wherever they wish without being accompanied by their husbands or relatives. This view applies a general statement to a special group on the basis of its intended meaning. Al-Shāfi'ī, on the other hand, says that in times of safety, a woman may travel alone and does not need a companion. She may be on her own with the travelling caravan and she will be safe.

In *al-Mudawwanah al-Kubrā* of Mālik's School we read: "I said: 'What does Mālik say concerning a woman who wants to go on pilgrimage but she has no guardian?' He replied: 'She goes with men and women whom she trusts.'"

## Mixing When Someone Dies

Mixing and conversation occur between people at a time when someone is dying or has departed life. The first thing that springs to mind in this connection is the offering of condolences, sharing sorrow and prayer that God may accept the deceased and bestow mercy on him or her. Furthermore, people counsel the family of the deceased to accept the event with resignation and patience and also to refrain from anything that Islam censures, such as wailing and lamenting.

Usāmah ibn Zayd narrated: "One of the Prophet's daughters sent him a message saying that a son of hers was dying and requested him to come over. He replied offering his greetings of peace and said: 'To God belongs all that He has taken and all that He has given. Everything is determined by Him at its time. Be patient and resign yourself to God's will, seeking His reward.' She sent back appealing to him to come over. He stood up to go to her, and with him went Sa'd ibn 'Ubādah, Mu'ādh ibn Jabal, Ubayy ibn Ka'b, Zayd ibn Thābit and others. The little boy was lifted up to the Prophet, as he was in the throes of death, twisting like a dry rag. The Prophet's eyes were tearful. Sa'd asked him: 'How come, Messenger of God?' The Prophet said: 'This is an expression of the feeling of mercy God has placed in the hearts of His servants. God bestows mercy on those of His servants who are merciful.'" (Related by al-Bukhari and Muslim)

In his commentary, Ibn Ḥajar says: "This hadith highlights several interesting points including... the permissibility of going to offer condolences and visiting the sick without the need for prior permission." Ibn Ḥajar is referring here to the fact that a number of the Prophet's companions went with him.

Jābir ibn 'Abdullāh reports: "When my father was killed, I kept removing the cover off his face and weeping. People around me were telling me not to do so, but the Prophet said nothing. My father's sister also wept. The Prophet said to her: 'You may weep or may not. The angels were shading him with their wings until you lifted his body.'" (Related by al-Bukhari and Muslim)

When a person dies, the body is prepared for burial. It is washed thoroughly and wrapped in shrouds. This is another time when men and women may have to be together and help one another. Umm ʿAṭiyyah of Anṣār says: "When the Prophet's daughter died, he came in to us [i.e. the women attending her] and said: 'Wash her body three times, or five, or more if you wish, and use water mixed with lotus. In the last wash add some camphor. When you have finished, let me know.' When we completed what he said, we informed him. He gave us his top garment and said: 'As you wrap her, make this one next to her body.'" In another version, the Prophet said to them: "Start with her right side and with the organs you wash when you do the ablution." (Related by al-Bukhari and Muslim)

When the deceased has been prepared for burial, it is time to offer the Funeral, i.e. *Janāẓah* Prayer for him or her, and this is something that both men and women can join in. ʿĀ'ishah narrated: "When Saʿd ibn Abi Waqqāṣ died, the Prophet's wives sent a message that his funeral should come into the mosque to allow them to offer the prayer for the deceased. The funeral procession came in and paused by their quarters as they performed the *Janāzah* Prayer for him." (Related by Muslim)

In the context of explaining how the Prophet's funeral was conducted, Imam al-Nawawī says: "The fact confirmed by the majority of scholars is that his companions offered the *Janāzah* Prayer for him individually. A group of men would come in, pray individually, and then leave to allow others to come in and do the same. Women went in to do the same after the men had finished. Then children did the same."

Again, in *al-Mudawwanah al-Kubrā* of the Mālikī School of *Fiqh* we read: "I asked: 'According to Mālik, do women offer the *Janāzah* Prayer?' He said: 'Yes, they do.'" In *al-Mabsūṭ* by al-Sarakhsī: "Women form their rows in *Janāzah* Prayer behind men's rows, as the Prophet says: 'The best of women rows are the last.'"

There are different views on whether women may join the funeral procession as the deceased is taken to be buried. As we mention these, it should be remembered that if women join, they are in a procession which may include a large number of men and there may be some exchange of condolences and expressions of grief.

Umm ʿAṭiyyah says: "We were told not to join funeral processions, but without emphasis." (Related by al-Bukhari and Muslim) Ibn Ḥajar says: "The phrase, 'without emphasis', means that this order was not emphasised so as to put it alongside prohibited actions. Thus, she suggests that joining a funeral procession is discouraged, but not prohibited." Al-Qurṭubī says: "Taken at face value, what Umm ʿAṭiyyah has reported suggests that it is simply a question of discouragement, not prohibition." This is agreed upon by the majority of scholars. Mālik leans towards the view that it is permissible for women to join a funeral procession. This is indeed the view of the people of Madinah. Further evidence in support of its permissibility is found in the hadith related by Ibn Abi Shaybah and narrated by Abu Hurayrah: "The Prophet was walking in a funeral procession when ʿUmar saw a woman and shouted at her. the Prophet said to him: 'Leave her alone, ʿUmar...'" This hadith is also related by both Ibn Mājah and al-Nasāʾī through slightly different chains of transmission in which all reporters are classified as highly reliable.

*Al-Mudawwanah al-Kubrā* includes: "I asked: 'Did Mālik allow women to join funeral processions?' He answered: 'Yes. Mālik said there is no harm in a woman joining the funeral of her child or parent, or her husband or sister, if it is socially acceptable for a person like her to join such a funeral.'"

Ibn Daqīq al-ʿĪd says: "A number of hadiths are reported which speak strongly against women, or some of them, joining funeral processions. One example is a hadith concerning the Prophet's daughter, Fāṭimah. This may be specific to her because of her social status, while the aforementioned hadith narrated by Umm ʿAṭiyyah applies to women in general. Alternatively, we may say that the two hadiths refer to different situations women experience. Mālik considers it permissible for women to join such funerals, but he discourages young women doing it in situations where it is considered unbecoming." I may add here that the hadith that quotes the Prophet as saying to some women, "Go back with a burden and without reward," is lacking in authenticity.

In all cultures, visiting graveyards to remember deceased loved ones is encouraged. Islam encourages visiting graves and graveyards because it reminds us of death and Islam wants Muslims to always remember death and what comes after it. The question is whether this is done by men and women.

ʿĀ'ishah mentions that she asked the Prophet what she should do and say when she visited graves: "How do I address them, Messenger of God?" "He told me to say: 'Peace be to the dwellers of this place who were believers and Muslims. May God bestow His mercy on those of us who have already gone and those who remain. We shall be joining you when God wills.'" (Related by Muslim)

Anas ibn Mālik narrated: "The Prophet passed by a woman who was weeping by the side of a grave. He said to her: 'Fear God and be patient in adversity.'" (Related by al-Bukhari and Muslim)

Ibn Ḥajar comments: "The fact that al-Bukhari included the chapter heading 'Visiting Graveyards' indicates that it is permissible. He seems to refrain from expressly stating this because scholars held different views on the matter. Al-Bukhari appears not to consider those hadiths that express such permissibility as meeting his conditions of authenticity. Muslim relates on Buraydah's authority a hadith abrogating the prohibition of visiting graveyards. It states: 'I had prohibited visiting graveyards. Now you better visit them...'

Muslim also relates on Abu Hurayrah's authority that the Prophet said: 'Visit graves because they remind you of death...' Different views are expressed concerning women. Scholars say that the later verdict of permissibility applies to them. This is the view of the majority and it applies in normal situations when nothing untoward is feared.

Further evidence of permissibility is found in the above hadith reported by Anas which is entered under al-Bukhari's heading of 'Visiting Graveyards.' The hadith is clear because the Prophet did not object to the woman's presence by the side of the grave. When the Prophet approved of a situation, his approval counts as clear evidence. Among those who consider the Prophet's permission to apply to both men and women is 'Ā'ishah. Al-Ḥākim related on Ibn Abi Mulaykah's authority that he saw her visiting the grave of her brother, 'Abd al-Raḥmān. "She was asked: 'Did not the Prophet prohibit such visits?' She answered: 'Yes, he did, but he subsequently encouraged visiting graves.'" It is also suggested that the subsequent permission applies to men only, while women are not allowed to visit graveyards. This is the view clearly supported by Abu Isḥāq in *al Muhadhdhab*. He cites a hadith narrated by 'Abdullāh ibn 'Amr and another related by al-Tirmidhī on Abu Hurayrah's authority quoting the Prophet as saying: "God curses women who frequently visit graves."

Ibn Ḥajar further adds: "Those who maintain that visiting graveyards is discouraged for women also differ as to whether the discouragement is of the easier or stricter type. Al-Qurṭubī says: 'The curse applies only to those who do it too often as indicated in the phraseology of the hadith. Perhaps the reason is that such frequent visits lead to the negligence of a woman's duties towards her husband and family and because of the lamentation they often do. Hence, it may be said that when all such undesirables are refrained from, visiting graves becomes permissible, because both men and women need to be reminded of death...' This hadith provides a clear indication of the Prophet's humility with all people, his lenient approach towards those who are unaware, his forbearance with people who are in distress and his acceptance of their excuses. It also indicates that he always enjoined good action and counselled against what is unacceptable... Scholars take it as evidence of the permissibility of visiting graves, whether the visitor is male or female and the visited person a Muslim or not, because no inquiry of such identity is mentioned in the hadith. Al-Nawawī adds that such permissibility is agreed upon by the majority of scholars."

## Taking Up Matters with Leaders

In an Islamic society, even the overall leader of a country remains accessible to people who may need to put to him their problems or seek his advice. In modern urban societies people need to go to officials and employees of different positions in order to attend to their interests. In such cases, mixing, discussion and even argument may be necessary and any of this can happen between men and women. The Qur'an tells us of the case of the woman who went to the Prophet and argued with him about her situation when her husband uttered words that were common during pre-Islamic days but which Islam prohibits. This event, however, occurred before such prohibition. The Qur'an mentions that God listened to this woman's complaint and the way she argued with the Prophet. He then said: "God has heard the words of the woman who pleads with you concerning her husband, and complained to God. God has heard what you both had to say. God hears all and sees all." (58: 1)

Women used to go to the Prophet seeking answers to their problems. Later, they went to caliphs and governors. Ka'b ibn Mālik gives a detailed account of the three people, including himself, who were left to await God's judgement as they did not join the Prophet on the Expedition of Tabuk. His account includes: "Hilāl ibn Umayyah's wife went to the Prophet and said: 'Messenger of God! Hilāl is an elderly person who has no servant. Would you dislike that I should serve him?' He said: 'That is all right, provided that he does not come near you.' She said: 'By God! He has no motivation to anything. He has not stopped weeping ever since this thing happened.'" (Related by al-Bukhari and Muslim)

'Ā'ishah narrated: "Fāṭimah [the Prophet's daughter] and al-'Abbās [his uncle] went to Abu Bakr asking for their inheritance from the Prophet. They wanted to have their shares of his land in Fadak and their portion of the gains of Khaybar. Abu Bakr said to them: 'I heard the Prophet as he said: "We do not bequeath any inheritance. Whatever we leave behind goes to charity. Muhammad's household can only eat of this property." I will most certainly do with this property everything I saw the Prophet doing.' Fāṭimah never spoke to him again until she died." (Related by al-Bukhari and Muslim)

It is clear that Fāṭimah felt that she had a right to inherit from her father, like all Muslim women, but Abu Bakr implemented what he heard the Prophet saying about any property left by a prophet. It cannot be given to his heirs, but must be given away as charity. Because Fāṭimah was unaware of this fact, she felt that she had been denied what was due to her. Far be it from Abu Bakr to deny her anything that was owed to her. He was a model of uprightness and fairness. This hadith is cited here as an example of how women could put their case directly to a ruler without any hesitation.

Zayd ibn Aslam quotes a report by his father: "I went out to the market place with 'Umar ibn al-Khaṭṭāb. A young lady caught up with him and addressed him saying: 'My husband has died, leaving behind young boys. By God, they cannot feed themselves, and they have neither farming land nor productive cattle. I fear that a season of shortage may see them buried. I am the daughter of Khaffāf ibn Aymā' al-Ghifārī who was with the Prophet at al-Hudaybiyah.' 'Umar stopped to speak to her and then said: 'Welcome to one who is close to us.' He then went up to a strong camel which was tied at home, and loaded it with two sacks he filled with food. In between them he put some clothes and some money. He gave her the camel's lead and said: 'Take this home. It will not be exhausted before God has given you something better.' Someone said to him: '*Amīr al-Mu'minīn*, you have given her rather much!' 'Umar said: 'How ill you say! I saw this woman's father and brother besieging a fort for a time before they overpowered its defenders. The following morning we were calculating our shares of the booty we gained from it.'" (Related by al-Bukhari)

Again, this is a case of woman approaching the caliph directly, seeking his help, identifying herself and putting her case succinctly to him. She does this in the open market, with people around. No one thinks ill of her for doing so. On the contrary, the caliph's help was immediately forthcoming, together with a promise of further help in due course. The only question raised was whether the help granted immediately was right or excessive.

## Pleading Someone's Case

We have texts speaking of occasions when mixing with and speaking to members of the opposite sex occur in order to plead someone else's case, or in trying to bring about a compromise solution to a lingering problem.

'Ā'ishah narrated: "I bought a slave woman called Barīrah, but her people made it a condition that they retained her loyalty. I mentioned this to the Prophet and he said: 'Set her free. Loyalty belongs to the one who pays the money.' I set her free. The Prophet called her in and gave her the choice to stay with her husband or to leave him.[11]

11. Since she became a free woman while her husband was a slave, their marriage was dissolved unless she opted to retain it. Hence the Prophet offered her a choice. – Editor's note.

She said: 'If he would give me so much, I would not stay with him.' She chose to be free." Ibn 'Abbās says: "Barīrah's husband was a slave named Mughīth. I can almost see him walking behind her, weeping so much as to wet his beard with his tears. The Prophet said to his uncle: ''Abbās! Do you not wonder how much Mughīth loves Barīrah and how she dislikes him?' The Prophet said to her: 'Would you consider going back to him?' She asked him: 'Messenger of God, are you bidding me?' He said: 'I am only pleading his case.' She said: 'I have no need for him.'" (Related by al-Bukhari)

Anas narrated that "Umm Ḥārithah, al-Rubayyi''s sister, injured someone. His people complained to the Prophet. He said: 'Just retribution applies.' Al-Rubayyi''s mother said: 'Messenger of God! Would she be subjected to retribution? By God, she will not be subjected to it.' The Prophet said: 'Limitless is God in His glory! Umm al- Rubayyi', just retribution is the law stated in God's Book.' She replied: 'By God, just retribution will never be exacted against her.' She hardly had moved when those people accepted indemnity. The Prophet said: 'Among God's servants are some whose appeal He would grant should they appeal to Him with an oath.'" (Related by Muslim)

The principle of just retribution in Islamic law stipulates an eye for an eye, etc. and that injuries are matched with their like. The Prophet wanted to apply this principle in this case, but the woman's mother objected, swearing by God that her daughter would not be subjected to this. God accepted her oath, making the people concerned accept financial compensation.

'Ā'ishah narrated that a woman committed theft during the Prophet's lifetime... Her people implored Usāmah ibn Zayd to appeal to the Prophet to show clemency. When Usāmah spoke to the Prophet, his face changed colour. The Prophet reproached him saying: "Are you appealing against a mandatory punishment prescribed by God?" (Related by al-Bukhari and Muslim) In Muslim's version, the following is added: "She was brought to God's Messenger, and then Usāmah ibn Zayd appealed to him." Ibn Ḥajar comments that Muslim's version indicates that the proper way to appeal for clemency is that it should be in the presence of the person concerned, so that he knows that the appeal was made and rejected.

## Mixing When Prosecuting a Legal Case

### 1. Acting as a witness

God says in the Qur'an: "Call in two of your men to act as witnesses, but if two men are not available, then a man and two women, whom you consider acceptable as witnesses, so that if either of them should make a mistake, the other will remind her." (2: 282) Imam Ibn al-Qayyim says: "It is more likely that women are present at a time when a divorced couple remarry than their presence at the time when documents and deeds of loan are executed. Likewise, they are more likely to be present when a will is written down before one's death. Since God has accepted them as witnesses in cases of loan agreements, even though they are often made in male company, their acceptance as witnesses in situations where they are more likely to be present, such as wills and marriages, is perfectly acceptable."

### 2. Testifying

In her account of the story of falsehood,[12] 'Ā'ishah said: "When people spoke about me as they did... the Prophet came to my home and questioned my maid about me. She said: 'By God, I know of no fault in her, except that she might lie down and sleep. A sheep may come then and eat her dough.' Some of his companions spoke roughly to the maid, saying: 'Tell the truth to the Prophet.' They

12. The Story of Falsehood refers to the rumour started by some hypocrites falsely accusing 'Ā'ishah of adultery. Her innocence is stated in the Qur'an, Surah 24, Verses 11-20. - Editor's note.

pressed her, stating to her what was being said against her mistress. She said: 'All glory be to God! By Him I know nothing about her other than what a goldsmith knows of his pure gold.'" (Related by al-Bukhari and Muslim)

### 3. Filing a Lawsuit and Issuing a Verdict

Anas reports: "Umm Ḥārithah, al-Rubayyi''s sister injured someone. His people complained to the Prophet. He said: 'Just retribution applies.'" (Related by Muslim)

Jābir narrated that a woman from the Makhzūm clan of the Quraysh committed theft. When she was brought in to the Prophet, she appealed to his wife, Umm Salamah, to intercede for her. The Prophet said: "By God! If it were Fāṭimah, I would still cut her hand..." (Related by Muslim)

Sa'īd ibn Zayd reports that Arwā complained to Marwān against him, alleging that he usurped something that was rightfully hers. He said: "Would I short-change her in what is rightfully hers? I testify that I heard the Prophet as he said: 'Whoever takes away a little spot of land unfairly will on the Day of Judgement be collared with it to the depths of seven earths.'" (Related by al-Bukhari and Muslim)

In all these cases we note that parties to the case spoke to each other and were together when the case was considered. The people involved in each case were men and women. Nothing was expressed against their being together.

### 4. Exacting punishment

God says in the Qur'an: "As for the adulteress and the adulterer, flog each of them with a hundred stripes, and let not compassion for them keep you from [carrying out] this law of God, if you truly believe in God and the Last Day; and let a number of believers witness their punishment." (24: 2)

Abu Hurayrah and Zayd ibn Khālid al-Juhanī narrated: "A man came to the Prophet and said to him: 'I appeal to you by God to judge between us according to God's Book.' His opponent, who was more learned, stood up and said: 'He makes a fair request. Please judge between us according to God's Book, but let me speak first.' The Prophet told him to say what he wanted. He said: 'My son was working for this man and he committed adultery with his wife. I settled the case with him by giving him 100 sheep and a servant. I then asked some learned people and they told me that my son's punishment is 100 lashes and that he be sent into exile for a year, while this man's wife is to be stoned.' The Prophet said: 'By Him who holds my soul in His hand, I will judge between you two according to God's Book: the sheep and the servant are to be returned to you. Your son is to be whipped 100 lashes and sent into exile for a year. You, Unays, go to this man's wife and ask her. If she confesses her guilt, then stone her.' She admitted her guilt and she was stoned." (Related by al-Bukhari and Muslim)

'Abdullāh ibn 'Umar quotes the Prophet as saying: "...God does not punish anyone for weeping or feeling their grief. He punishes for what this [pointing to his tongue] may say, or He may bestow His mercy. A deceased person suffers when his relatives wail for his death." 'Umar used to beat people who do it with his stick, or throw stones or dust at them. (Related by al-Bukhari and Muslim)

## Exchanging Appeals to God

God says in the Qur'an: "The case of Jesus in the sight of God is the same as the case of Adam. He created him of dust and then said to him: 'Be,' and he was. This is the truth from your Lord: be not, then, among the doubters. If anyone should dispute with you about this [truth] after all the knowledge you have received, say: Come. Let us summon our sons and your sons, our women and your women, and ourselves and yourselves; then let us pray humbly and solemnly and invoke God's curse upon the ones who are telling a lie." (3: 59-61)

Commenting on the last of these verses, Ibn Kathīr says: "Let us summon...means that both parties should bring their women and children... The following morning the Prophet came with his grandchildren al-Ḥasan and al-Ḥusayn, covering them with his overcoat, while Fāṭimah walked behind him, ready for the exchange of appeals. At the time, he was married to several women..." This was an occasion when the Prophet proposed to Najrān delegation making this mutual appeal to God, bringing with them their women and children so that they would all share in the appeal.

## Interesting Occasions of Mixing

### In Jest or Earnest

Islam encourages competitions and rivalry when these do not involve anything forbidden. This may involve women's participation, either as participants or observers, as is clear in the following example:

Abu Ḥamīd al-Sā'idī narrated: "We joined the Prophet on the Expedition of Tabuk. When he arrived at Wādi al-Qurā, we saw a woman in her garden. The Prophet said to his companions: 'Guess the amount of dates she has [in her garden].' The Prophet guessed that it would be 10 *wisqs*.[13] He then said to the woman: 'Calculate the yield of your garden.' When he returned to Wādi al-Qurā on his way back, he asked the woman: 'How much did your garden yield?' She said: '10 *wisqs*. Just as God's Messenger guessed.'" (Related by al-Bukhari and Muslim)

13. *Wisq* was a recognized measure, which is equal to sixty *ṣā'*s, and a *ṣā'* is the fill of a man's cupped hands four times. – Editor's note.

The women witnessed this sort of exchange which was neither serious nor frivolous. This is not strange. We have seen how 'Ā'ishah watched the Abyssinian delegation dancing their folk dances in the Prophet's mosque. That was mere fun.

### Some Entertainment

Masrūq narrated: "We visited 'Ā'ishah and we found Ḥassān ibn Thābit there reciting a poem of his in which he says of 'Ā'ishah: 'She is chaste, mature and can never be accused of infidelity. She never says a word accusing women when they are unaware.' 'Ā'ishah said to him: 'But you are unlike that.' Masrūq said to her: 'Why do you permit him to visit you when God has said, "Awesome suffering awaits the one who took on himself the lead among them."' (24: 11) She said: 'What suffering is greater than being blind? Yet he used to defend God's Messenger with his poetry.'" (Related by al-Bukhari and Muslim)

Sa'd ibn Abi Waqqāṣ narrated: "'Umar sought permission to enter the Prophet's home when he had some women from the Quraysh who spoke to him loudly asking him for more. When 'Umar sought entry, they hurried to cover themselves. The Prophet admitted him and he was smiling. 'Umar said: 'May God make you always smile, Messenger of God.' The Prophet said: 'I have been wondering at these women who rushed to cover themselves when they heard your voice.' 'Umar said: 'They should have feared you more.' Turning to them, he said: 'You enemies of your own souls! Do you fear me and not fear God's Messenger?' They said: 'Yes; you are harsher than God's Messenger.' The Prophet said to him: 'By Him Who holds my soul in His hand, when Satan sees you taking one way, he will take a different way.'" (Related by al-Bukhari and Muslim)

### Listening to Good News

Abu Mūsā narrated: "... When the Prophet came in, Asmā' bint 'Umays said to him: 'Prophet of God! 'Umar said this and that.' He asked her what she said to him. When she told him, he said: 'He has no greater claim to me than you have. He and his companions have migrated once, but you, the people of the boat, have migrated twice.'" She said: "Abu Mūsā and the other people who travelled by boat came to me, one group after another, asking me about this hadith. Nothing in the world ever gave them greater pleasure or gratification than what the Prophet said concerning them." Asmā' also said: "Abu Mūsā would fain ask me to repeat this hadith to him." (Related by al-Bukhari and Muslim)

All these situations are subject to the Islamic rule which distinguishes between what is forbidden outright and its prohibition applies in all cases, and what is discouraged or prohibited for a particular reason. When such reason does not apply, then the discouragement or prohibition is similarly inapplicable. To give an example: easy conversation between men and women and watching certain male games are discouraged for fear that they may lead to temptation. When such temptation is totally out of the question, the discouragement does not apply.

## Muslim Men Meeting Non-Muslim Women

### During the Believers' Plight

The following hadith, narrated by Jundab ibn Sufyān, refers to an event from the early days of Islam in Makkah: "The Prophet was taken ill, so he did not perform his night worship on two or three nights. A woman came to him and said: 'Muhammad! I hope that your jinnee has deserted you. I have not seen him coming near you for two or three nights.' Soon afterwards Surah 93 was revealed, starting with: 'By the bright morning hours, and the night when it grows still and dark, your Lord has neither forsaken you, nor does He hate you.'" (93: 1-3) (Related by al-Bukhari and Muslim)

## To Criticise Sinful Practices and Establish Facts

Abu Dharr narrated: "Our people, the Ghifār, used to violate the restrictions applicable in the consecrated months. I set out with my brother, Unays, and our mother... When we arrived in Makkah I spoke to a man from there who looked weak. I asked him: 'Where is this man whom you call *Ṣābi'*?'[14] He pointed to me and shouted: 'This man is a *Ṣābi'*.' All people around came against me throwing at me every piece of dry mud and bone they could lay their hands on, until I lost consciousness... Then, on a bright night with a full moon, I noticed that the people of Makkah were asleep and none of them was doing the *ṭawāf* around the Ka'bah. Two women were praying to the two idols Isāf and Nā'ilah. As the two women passed me during their *ṭawāf*, I said to them: 'Let these two copulate with each other.' They did not stop praying to them. I said: 'The one has a penis as hard as wood.' [I used the more vulgar word] They ran away wailing: 'If only some of our people were here.' Soon the Prophet met them..." (Related by Muslim)

The hadith continues: "Soon the Prophet met them as he was coming down with Abu Bakr. He asked what the matter was with them. They said: 'It is that *Ṣābi'* standing behind the coverings of the Ka'bah.' He asked them what he said to them. They replied: 'He said a mouthful.' The Prophet came down until he kissed the Black Stone and did the *ṭawāf* with his companion. When he completed his prayer, I was the first to greet him with the Islamic greeting. I said: 'Peace be to you, Messenger of God.' He said: 'And to you be peace together with God's mercy. Who are you?' I said: 'A man from Ghifār...'" (Related by Muslim)

Abu Dharr seems to have wanted to take some revenge against the Quraysh for the treatment he had received earlier. Hence, when he

14. *Ṣābi'* means 'deserter.' The idolater Arabs used to refer to the Prophet and his companions as deserters, because they abandoned their pagan practices and adopted Islam.

saw the two women paying homage to these idols, he said what he said, using vulgar language and referring to the legend connected with Isāf and Nā'ilah. The legend says that they were a man and a woman who came to Makkah to worship at the Ka'bah, but as they were doing the *ṭawāf*, Isāf, the man, bent over the woman and kissed her. The *ṭawāf* is an act of worship performed at the most sacred of places. His action profaned the place and the worship. Hence, as the legend goes, both were cast into stone. The Quraysh made them idols and placed them in the Ka'bah close to al-Safa. They remained there until Makkah fell to Islam when all idols were broken and the Ka'bah was cleared of them.

### During a Battle

Al-Barā' narrated: "We met the unbelievers on that day, [the day of the Battle of Uhud]. The Prophet positioned a company of archers, giving their command to 'Abdullāh [ibn Jubayr] and said to them: 'Do not leave your positions. If you see us winning, stay where you are, and if you see them winning, do not come to our help.' When the fighting started, the unbelievers were put to flight. I saw their women running up the mountain, having lifted their skirts. I could see their anklets..." (Related by al-Bukhari)

Ibn Ḥajar says: "Ibn Isḥāq gives a report by al-Zubayr ibn al-'Awwām who says: 'I saw Hind bint 'Utbah and her friends, having lifted their skirts and being put to flight.'"

### In Court

'Abdullāh ibn 'Umar narrated: "A group of Jews came to the Prophet and told him that a man and a woman from among them committed adultery. The Prophet asked them: 'What does the Torah say concerning the punishment of stoning?' They said: 'It mentions that their offence should be publicized and that they should be punished by flogging.' 'Abdullāh ibn Sallām said to them: 'You lie. It specifies the punishment of stoning.' They brought the Torah and opened it. One of them covered the verse speaking about stoning with his hand, reading what preceded it and what came after it. 'Abdullāh ibn Sallām said to him: 'Remove your hand.' When he did, the verse specifying stoning was read. The Jews said: 'Muhammad! He tells the truth. It states stoning.' The Prophet gave his instructions that the offenders should be stoned, which was done.[15] I saw the man bending over the woman to protect her." (Related by al-Bukhari and Muslim)

'Abdullāh ibn Sallām was a highly respected Jewish rabbi, and when the Prophet migrated to Madinah, he recognized him as the last of God's messengers. So he believed in him declaring himself a Muslim. He was present on this occasion and he exposed the tricks of those who wished not to implement the law contained in their scriptures.

## Requesting and Rendering Help

Abu Sa'īd al-Khudrī narrated: "We were travelling and we encamped at some place. A maid came to us and said: 'The chief of these quarters has been bitten by something, and our people are away. Is there among you anyone who can use a supplication to help?' [One version of this hadith mentions that the Muslim travellers requested some hospitality from those people but they declined.] A man went with her and prayed for the bitten man. He soon recovered and ordered that 30 sheep be given to the man and he gave us milk to drink. When our fellow came back, we asked him whether he (who had helped) used to do such prayers for healing. He said: 'No. I only read the Opening Surah of the Qur'an, *al-Fātiḥah*.' We advised each other not to do anything until we had asked the Prophet. When we arrived in Madinah, we mentioned what happened to the Prophet.

---

15. The Prophet ruled in this case as the Torah states the punishment. Both man and woman were given the same punishment of stoning, because they were both married. In the earlier case, where only the woman was stoned, it was because she was married while her partner was not.

He said: 'How could he tell that it was a special prayer for healing? Divide the gift among yourselves and give me a share.'" (Related by al-Bukhari and Muslim)

The point in this hadith is that the Prophet's companion went with the maid to see the chief. None of the Prophet's companions present objected to this. Nor did the Prophet express any disapproval of his action. On the contrary, he indicated that it was proper, as he wanted a share of the gift.

### With Captives

Iyās ibn Salamah quotes a report by his father who said: "We were sent on an expedition to fight the tribe of Fazārah and the Prophet appointed Abu Bakr as our commander. When we were about an hour's march from their water springs, he told us to stop for a rest. He then launched the attack on the people by the spring, killing some and taking others captives. I could see a group of people including children. I thought that they might get to the mountain before me and seek refuge there. I aimed an arrow between them and the mountain. When they saw it, they stopped. I took them captive and brought them in. Among them was a woman from Fazārah wearing an old leather dress and her daughter who was very beautiful was with her. I took them to Abu Bakr, who gave me the daughter as my share of the war gains. When we arrived in Madinah, I had not lifted her clothes. The Prophet saw me in the market place and he said to me: 'Salamah, give me the woman as a gift.' I said: 'Messenger of God. I certainly like her, but I have not lifted a dress she wears.' The Prophet saw me again at the market the following day. He again said to me: 'Salamah, give me the woman as a gift. May God reward you and your father.' I said: 'She is yours, Messenger of God, and I have not lifted a dress she wears.' The Prophet sent her to the people of Makkah in exchange for some Muslims who had been taken captive by the unbelievers there." (Related by Muslim)

Anas ibn Mālik narrated: "A Jewish woman brought the Prophet a poisoned sheep and he ate of it. The woman was brought in to him and some people asked him: 'Shall we kill her?' He said: 'No.' I continued to see the traces of that food in the Prophet's mouth."[16] (Related by al-Bukhari and Muslim)

## In Sound Dreams

The reason we are including meeting between men and women in dreams is that a dream by a prophet is true. 'Ā'ishah said: "The first aspect of revelation given to God's Messenger was that he saw true dreams in his sleep." (Related by al-Bukhari and Muslim) The Prophet is also quoted as saying: "A dream by a believer is one out of forty-six portions of prophethood." (Related by al-Bukhari and Muslim)

From another point of view, we want to draw attention to the fact that for men and women to meet is a natural thing. Those who impose restrictions on themselves taking measures to avoid such meetings, through which God tests them when awake, cannot avoid it in sleep. This is a permanent test which they have to face willingly or unwillingly, with Muslim or non-Muslim women, either when awake or asleep.

'Ā'ishah narrated that the Prophet said to her: "I was shown you twice in my sleep. I saw you wrapped in silk, and I was told, 'This is your wife.' I lifted the cover and I saw you. I thought, 'If this is from God, He will accomplish it.'" (Related by al-Bukhari and Muslim)

16. This is a very short version of a longer ḥadīth that gives details of the Prophet's eating of the poisoned sheep. One of His companions named Bishr also ate of the lamb and he died of poisoning. When the Prophet questioned her, she said to him that she thought that if he were truly a Prophet, he would be informed by God and he would not come to any harm. If he were an impostor, she would thus rid the world of him. Reports differ about her fate.

Abu Hurayrah narrated: "We were with the Prophet when he said: 'As I was asleep, I saw myself in heaven. I saw a woman performing the ablution close to a palace. I asked whose palace it was, and I was told that it belonged to 'Umar. I remembered how jealous he was and I turned back.' 'Umar wept and said: 'Would I be jealous of you, Messenger of God?'" (Related by al-Bukhari and Muslim)

Umm al-'Alā' said: "... I also saw in my dream a flowing spring belonging to 'Uthmān. I went to the Prophet and mentioned this to him. He said: 'This is his good action, flowing for him.'" (Related by al-Bukhar.)

Ibn Ḥajar says: "Ibn Baṭṭāl states that scholars are unanimous that the Prophet's statement about the dream of a true believer being a portion of prophethood also applies to dreams by women believers."